RAGE
WITHIN

Trevor Hercules

The X Press

Published by
The X Press
PO Box 25694
London N17 6FP
Tel: 020 8801 2100
Fax: 020 8885 1322
E-mail: vibes@xpress.co.uk
Website: www.xpress.co.uk

First Edition 2006

Printed by Bookmarque Ltd., Croydon, UK

Distributed in the UK by Turnaround Distribution
Unit 3, Olympia Trading Estate, Coburg Road, London N22 6TZ
Tel: 020 8829 3000
Fax: 020 8881 5088

Distributed in the U.S. by National Book Network
15200 NBN Way, Blue Ridge, PA 17214
Tel: 717 794 3800
Fax: 717 794 3804

ISBN: 1-902934-36-9

For all those who've gone through life with others saying they will amount to nothing.
Just believe, and keep hope alive.

ONE

9th October 2000

As I sit here in this empty flat in south London, with a gun in my hand contemplating my life and all that's gone before, I know very soon I will rise, go out and find the man I'm going to kill; the man who disrespected me and questioned my manhood. Let me tell you how it all began; how I managed to reach this point, the place of no return. As you know, every story has a beginning:

My name is Trevor Hercules-Ledwidge. I was born in St Mary's Hospital, Paddington, London. Most of my life - as far back as I can remember - I've spent in children's homes up and down the country. The fact that they were Catholic homes has had profound influence on my life. I was brought up as a Roman Catholic, with all the values that exist within Catholicism. (Oh, and by the way I'm black.)

I was an altar boy, a very good one I may add, if there is such a thing. I remember getting up at six a.m. to serve mass during the week and in the evening I helping out at Benediction. Those years were filled with a tranquil serenity, yet something was missing. Deep down I was sad. I was unable to put my finger on it, because at that time I hadn't a clear picture of myself. I remember many times taking myself off somewhere isolated and having a cry. And there were many times, after lights out, that I lay down in my bed and the tears would just roll down my cheeks.

Once in a blue moon my mother would appear and take me out for the afternoon. One of the priests or nuns would say, "Your mother's coming today." I would get into my Sunday best. Then I'd be walked to the secluded part of the building where visitors came. We never came here, unless we had a visit from relatives. It was annexed, from the main building and it always seemed strange to me. I remember always feeling tense and nervous. And then this exotic, sunny spirited, black lady would appear and give me and my brother a hug. Then we'd be on our way.

She took us into town, bought us sweets and things. I don't recall any meaningful conversations but I remember she smiled a lot. The visits always seemed over far too soon. Then it was back to the home, back to what I knew. And I could never remember it being any other way.

The one question that remained with me throughout those years was, *Why am I here*? At even the most strange and bizarre moments I'd sometimes just look around me and feel so out of place. This sense would just wash over me and I'd think, *I don't belong here*. Often it was like I was on the outside looking in.

The last children's home I went to - St. Francis, in Bedfordshire -was a huge monolith of a building with a big central, concrete yard. You'd cross the yard, walk down the side of one of the buildings and enter out into a wonderful open field with goal posts at either end and a river running alongside. Behind the farthest goal post was an uneven field with a large overhanging tree which gave wonderful shade during hot summer days.

The home was run by two priests and three male workers who lived in. There were several nuns about the place who dealt mainly with the kitchens and pantry, or in some capacity in and around the church, which was located on the grounds.

I say it was a huge building, but in fact, it had many segments. There were several detached buildings within that one building and from the outside, you would never know how vast the place was. The entrance was a large gate, on not what you would call a busy road, but a public road; a road which had several shops. Once inside the road couldn't be seen. It was like we were banged up in prison, and what took place inside, those outside could not see and wouldn't know. What we *did* see of the outside world we saw mostly through our coach window on the way to, or from, school. And as you can imagine, sitting by the window was highly prized.

Each school day the dilapidated coach would arrive and pick us up inside the gate. Then, it was straight off to school where it parked right outside. We went straight in, watched by the driver. God help anyone who missed that coach whether it be in the mornings, or after school, where it waited for us and was never late.

Institutions, especially Catholic institutions run by nuns and priests, were very strict. Yet despite the lack of freedom, and unlike most children, we loved going to school. It was a chance to mix and be with other people. But most of all it was a chance to get away; to get away from the male workers who made our lives a misery, particularly McCann. Shamus McCann. A short, squat, bearded man from Scotland who made our lives hell—especially mine.

And anywhere I see you McCann, anywhere. I will SMASH you, I will BEAT you. I will STOMP on you......
Thirty years on and still the anger had not subsided.

I LOOKED DOWN into my lap where I held the nine millimetre gun. It had been my companion for many years, even in my darkest times when I became a bum and could have used the money most. I never once thought of selling it.

It usually felt cold when I handled it– detached from me. It was as if we both had jobs to do, as if we had been given orders to carry out and came together solely for that purpose. But today the gun felt warm and somehow sensual– an extension of me. I could almost hear the gun whisper, "Don't worry, I'm your friend, I'm your best friend. Where are all those other so-called friends when you need them? We don't need anyone else. We'll take care of this guy together, you and I. Don't worry. We'll end his life *forever*."

I was happy, and I laughed aloud. *Madness* - who always urged me on to stick up for myself, to get even, to avenge any liberty regardless of cost - ran amok in my brain, screaming about Judgement Day, going to the well, drinking blood, and ripping out hearts. Again, I laughed aloud. But this time *Madness* joined in with me, and we laughed and we laughed. *Madness* I knew now, was my best friend, as I'd always known deep down inside. He bullied and shouted and screamed at me, and even when others were frightened to stand up for who and what they were, *Madness* always forced me to stand proud and tall at being black and never to be ashamed.

Though it was the voice of my inner conscience, I called it '*Madness*' because at times it was much safer to keep my mouth shut and melt into the background, but *Madness* propelled me into the role of spokesman; made me say what others were afraid to say, and dare not say, even though they knew it to be true. Yes, *Madness* had been with me a long time; since the early days of my struggle to find my black identity. But somehow along the way, we gradually lost sight of the real issues. Our views and perceptions became distorted until we became a highly dangerous combination. A walking time bomb.

I put my gloves on, picked up the gun, and wiped it clean of fingerprints. It was a dark, cold October evening and the clock showed eight. I washed and creamed my face, combed my hair and put on my long black overcoat and my black woolly hat and gloves. I put the gun in the right hand pocket of my coat. It felt heavy, but not unduly so; it's a feel, a weight, that I'm comfortable with. Trance-like, I went through the motions; passed the wardrobe mirror, stopped to look at myself, and quickly moved on. I didn't want to see that cold individual staring back at me. Who is he? Where is Trevor?

I know Trevor has vanished. Fleetingly, I wonder if he will ever return. I remember the exact words relayed to me from a supposedly good friend of mine. "Peter says, 'Your gone, finished, Trevor.'" It had hurt me then, but those very words now haunted me.

I opened the cupboard, fiddled about at the back, and found the secret compartment. I took the plastic bag containing 35 nine millimetre bullets, and put them in my left hand pocket. As I did so, the tears began to roll down my cheeks. I know I will not be coming back. A testimony to how far I have fallen and let myself go. I don't even have a plan. All I know is that I am going to KILL that son of a bitch today. And God help anyone who gets in my way.

I opened the door and stepped outside into the cold night air. Through my tears, I silently mumbled, "God forgive me."

TWO

It was 1969. I can't remember the exact date I left the children's home for good but I remember the events of the day as though it were yesterday. I had turned fifteen. Everybody left the home at age fifteen, after the fourth year of secondary school. You had no choice, those were the rules, regardless of whether you wanted to stay on or not. Luckily, most of us couldn't wait to get out of that place.

On one hand, I was glad I was now about to be free of the claustrophobic, enclosed place that in essence was, to me, a prison. Yet on the other hand, I was slightly apprehensive about going out into the big wide world beyond the gates of the children's home. Because you see, I'd spent all my life in care, either in one children's home or another, always in an enclosed environment, always on the inside looking out. I had not been prepared for what lay ahead of me on my journey to adulthood.

Where the person who called herself my mother was, I had no idea. All I knew was that I was alone; on my own, sticking up for myself, fighting my own battles, and mostly finding out about life. I was given a few pounds and a ticket to London to meet my welfare officer, Mr. Logey, in Holland Park. On my arrival he informed me that my mother was in America and he seemed quite saddened by my lack of emotion and curiosity. He asked me to wait while he conferred with his colleagues in another room.

With no family and nowhere to go, they were stuck with me. And quite frankly they didn't seem prepared for this type of situation. They were very kind though and lots of women came bringing me sweets and other goodies while I waited. But on their faces and in their eyes I saw the sadness of my plight. And I felt ashamed, as if I'd done something wrong. I felt shame too, for the people that brought me into this world.

As those who came in to make me feel welcome and at home, silently without words or deeds left unsaid, what they were thinking about any parent who could subject their child to such as this.

Even now as I write this, I can still feel the prickles behind my eyes, and the hot flushes. And the shame, oh the shame. At that young age I knew that I was different, I knew I was black. But for the most part I wasn't conscious of it. Unless of course programmes such as "Until Death Do Us Part" with Alf Garnett running around shouting "Coons niggers wogs monkeys jungle bunnies" came on.

Imagine around thirty youngsters in a TV room with Alf Garnett screaming from the television "wog niggers and coons" and you being the only black kid. You just know that there's going to be lots of trouble. And so it was in the early days, and at school with the bigger boys. But it soon stopped, because I don't play that game, and I don't care how big you are.

And for the most part my life in the various children's homes which were incidentally were all in the country. I would say carried on quite normally. Being in the homes out in the country I believe I was shielded from a lot of racism. I was more likely in Bexhill, Sussex to encounter old dears' who would gush "What a lovely colour you are you look wonderful" and genuinely mean it. And later on they would turn up at the convent asking the Sisters if they could invite me to tea. All very quaint. Shefford in Bedfordshire was much the same, I was never really called names of a racial nature. But looking back I believed evil Shamus McCann was what we would now term a racist. So you see the matter of being black was never an issue to me behind the walls of those children 's homes.

I was shielded. We didn't really go out, and we weren't allowed to watch much telly. I didn't think of myself as a black or dark person. I was just me Trevor. But as I sat there in that welfare office on Holland Park road, surrounded by these sympathetic people. I remembered flashes of Alf Garnett coming to me. "Nigger coon black bastard".

I put my head in my hands and silently shed a tear

for myself and for my shame. But I made sure no one saw my tears.

After leaving me waiting for a few hours, Mr Logey finally came in with a woman I believed to be his supervisor. Rather dejectedly, she admitted that they were having difficulty placing me. It seemed they couldn't put me in a hostel, or didn't want to, because of my vulnerability. And the set-ups they had where you live in a house with staff members were either full, or only available for younger boys.

The final outcome as proposed by Mr Logey, was that I should stay at his home in Hampstead until they were able to find a place for me. Now-a-days I'm sure the authorities would never allow this, but Mr Logey was a good guy as far as I knew. And in any event, with regard to my physical safety, I felt quite capable of taking care of myself. As children in care, we were well aware that there were those in authority who tried to 'get hold of' young boys. In Saint Francis' there had been two incidents to my knowledge. One, I can still remember quite clearly:

It was a nice, hot, sunny day and it was a weekend. As usual we were bored. Many of us were out in the play yard lounging around and just taking it easy. One kid, let's just call him Brian, had gone for a drive with one of the new staff. When he returned, he came straight to the yard and declared that a new member of staff had pulled out his willy and tried to get him to touch it.

Now let me try to explain the trouble this could bring to Brian if he reported it. This was a Roman Catholic children's home and everyone here: staff, children, priests and nuns, were all Catholic. All of us kids on that yard knew that if he reported what had happened he was gonna be properly grilled and then called a liar. Father Ryan - the priest in charge - would be shouting and ranting words such as hellfire, devil, and damnation. Believe me, to go and report something like that wasn't going to be easy. But in the end, he did.

On that yard, that very day, we vowed that if something wasn't done we would do it ourselves. How, we had no idea. As the day wore on, we snatched pieces of information about what was happening; it wouldn't do to get caught standing around discussing it. You would surely be in trouble, then. Around evening time we saw the staff member who had done this dirty deed packing his things. He left as quietly as he came. Nothing happened, no proceedings, no fuss; life continued normally for all intents and purposes.

I looked across at Mr Logey and he looked as bent as a ten bob note, at least to my 15-year-old eyes. Greying hair, cravat and a slightly effeminate manner, he was a kindly man and the times he came to see or take me out he was all right. So I decided to go.

My worldly possessions were packed into a hold-all bag; just clothes, I had no pictures, no memorabilia, nothing of value, no roots– nothing. I had no father that I knew of, nor a mother for that matter. As I stood waiting for Mr Logey by the door with my hold-all at the ready, for the first time in my life I questioned who I really was.

Mr Logey came down, looked at me and said, "Don't worry, everything will work out." Maybe he could see that my whole life was confused and that after being in institutions for so long, to be let out into the real world with no experience or understanding of it, with no family, no friends, no one to go to or nowhere to go must be very daunting. Perhaps the fear he saw in my face provoked him to say those kind words.

With my bag in hand, we headed out into the night. Cars were whizzing past, lots of people were still about and there were neon lights everywhere.The place was so big. There was so much space and the cacophony of sound was music to my ears as I stared wide-eyed at everything I passed. This was all so new to me.

As I noted the hour, it was past my usual bedtime. But I had left Shefford and St. Francis behind me and it was now a new era. Again, I wondered what was to become of me. I put my hand in my pocket and felt the love letter that I had gotten from Anne, my 'girlfriend' in school. All at once a big smile came to my face. We had done nothing more than kiss, but at least I was warm in the knowledge that someone did care, someone did love me. A young girl about the same age as me, passed and smiled. I nodded my head. She wasn't as nice as Anne; Anne loved me.

We had found Mr Logey's car.

THREE

The cold October night was tinged with a briskness that invigorated me and made me feel good. I made my way to Stockwell station, changed at Brixton, and caught the Victoria line heading for Finsbury Park. The train wasn't quite full and I found myself a nice corner seat next to some dude who looked like a throwback from the sixties.

As I sat down he glanced at me, smiled, and nodded. I looked straight ahead, my face a cold, blank, mask. Not today, save that for someone who cares. Tonight I have no cares for you or anyone, not even myself.

The train stopped and two Jack-the-lads got on. They stood opposite and to the right hand side of me, holding onto the pole. They looked in my direction and I wilfully and purposefully stared straight into their faces. They shifted about uncomfortably, then moved along down the train. They deemed my challenge not for them– and they are right. Because there are times when you can feel danger and that its about, you don;t have to see it before it happens. Much of my life since leaving the children's home 'St. Francis' and coming to London has been filled with much anger. And a rage that burns deep within me.

AS I LEAVE THE STATION, the gun and the pocket which held it, felt warm. Heat radiated outward, as if the gun, nearing its target was trying to home in. Suddenly I was overwhelmed, as images of my life flashed before my eyes. Out of nowhere thoughts that had lain dormant, things I hadn't thought about for years, popped into my head; a point by point critique of my life. But I shook them loose and said quietly to myself, 'I am going to kill him, I am going to kill him.' And I was.

I stood on the other side of the road and looked at the pub where I knew he'd be. The pub was a modern day pub, with a big glass window that you could see through into a brightly lit interior. Two days had passed since I had been there. My first time, a man just passing in the night looking for a place to drown his sorrows and have a quiet drink. Then it turned nasty. People underestimating me, thinking I was a mug taking the piss. And to cap it all, spitting on me, one of the worst crimes of all. Didn't he know, he would have to die, if he let me walk out? Didn't he know there was no way I could let that go? The more I thought about the incident the hotter my blood boiled. My face and body burned. And *Madness* screamed, "Let's kill him now, let's kill him now, let's end his life once and for all, let's do it NOW."

I put the gun in my right hand and held it within my overcoat pocket. I walked across the road and straight through the swing doors. My heart was pounding, my chest was pounding, my ears were ringing. I looked neither right nor left. I pushed open the swing doors and walked to the back where the pool table was. I stood in the archway and surveyed the corner where the pool table stood. It was well lit.

The gun was halfway out of my pocket.

THIS IS IT.

I'm going to kill him now.

There he is!

But wait…. it wasn't him.

In fact, he wasn't there.

I checked all the faces again and again, he's wasn't fucking there. I strode around to the public bar. *Where is he? He's got to be here, but he's not. His two friends aren't even here.*

I felt a rage that I somehow managed to control. I exited the pub into the cold night air which direction I took I'm unable to tell you and found myself sitting on a bench staring at a small man-made pond. My body felt damp; I had been sweating profusely. My heart was still beating fast, but was beginning to slow. My ears adjusted. I could see two other couples on the other side of the pond sharing a bench and drunken revelry. As I regained my bearings I could see that the surrounding area was enclosed but it wasn't a park as such. It offered a modicum of cover from the main road but was planned in such a way that you could easily pass it and not know it was there. I took deep breaths, blew out slowly, and gradually got myself together.

I sat there a while and just pondered. Closing my eyes, I thought about what had happened those two days ago, about what had taken place for me to be where I was at this point, gun in pocket, ready to shoot and kill a man. A man that I had never set eyes on before that day.

It was a Tuesday and I had come up to Finsbury Park to see a friend I hadn't seen in years. His name was Leroy and we had done small bits of business over the years. Leroy always had something going on and always knew where to find a pound note. He had rung me up out of the blue and said we should meet up that day. I was glad to hear hid voice Leroy was about ten years younger than me and in the days when I was holding (had money), I always looked after him.

We met in some snazzy wine bar where he was on good terms with the proprietor. Over a bottle of wine, he outlined certain little scams he had on the go, saying there were certain little things he needed and wondered if, with my contacts, I could help him out. I explained that I had lost touch with many of my contacts - the truth of the matter was many of my contacts had let me go due to my unreliability and dabbling with drugs - but I assured him that I would be able to get the things he needed.

Throughout our meeting he studied me. Not slyly

or anything like that but openly and honestly, as a friend looking over an old friend. Just seeing where I was at. He didn't say it in so many words but what his reaction amounted to was, *Trevor your fucking up*. He had just bought a nice house and was driving one of the newest and latest model cars; he was expensively attired and very well groomed. He made several references to the old days and how it was and how I was. But the telling remark was when he said, "I remember when you used to give me money."

That kind of said it all. Here he was, upwardly mobile and there was me going down the ladder. He wasn't gloating at all, it was just a friendly observation of a friend who was genuinely concerned. We spoke of days gone by, how it used to be, how it was now, who was still around, who was in jail and who was dead. During the course of the conversation I realised how much Leroy had really looked up to me back in the day.

Eventually it came time to part, and as we approached Leroy's car he shoved a wad of notes into my hand. I declined his offer of a lift saying that I would make my own way back. He turned to me and gave me hug, something he had never done before. After arranging another meeting we said our goodbyes. Slowly, he manoeuvred his car out into the steady stream of traffic. It began to rain.

Long after his car had vanished, I just stood there staring. Suddenly becoming aware of the rain, I began to walk in what I thought was the direction of the train station. I counted the money he had given me; it was £500. Did I really look that bad? As I passed a shop window I glanced at myself, then stopped and had a good look. I felt compelled to see what Leroy had seen, I wanted to see the change in me. But I didn't really need to stop and look, I already knew; I already knew what Leroy saw, what others who had known me saw.

Always well-dressed and well-groomed, with money, a nice car and something going on; now I was wearing a pair of 'Mickey Mouse' shoes that weren't even leather, an overcoat that while not completely threadbare had seen better days, and a pair of slacks that were outdated and looked it. All-in-all the report card said: 'Trevor is going downhill and we see no sign of improvement'.

The sky above opened and unleashed a downpour. And as people scurried to and fro around me, I walked slowly, Leroy's words going around and around in my head, *"I remember when you used to give me money."*

The pub was a modern pub and it had a huge glass window that enabled you to see inside. I think I've already told you that, but never mind. Anyhow, it was a mixed pub but mainly black people. I stopped outside the huge plate of glass and peered in. It looked inviting and warm, a shelter from the rain. It had alcohol and was a place where a man could drown his sorrows and think back to what he was and not what he had become. A place where you could forget who you were for a time. A place where no one knew you. A place where no one knew you were a fuck-up and where no one even cared if you were. A place to rest.

I entered, went straight to the bar and ordered a double southern comfort and lemonade. I found myself in the vicinity of the pool table and found a nice little spot in the corner to watch proceedings. The pub was quite animated but not overly so. There was a mixture of young and old and there seemed to be a nice vibe to the place. I went to the bar several times for a variety of drinks and what with the wine, I was slowly getting drunk. Many thoughts ran through my head, too many to comprehend. At one stage I promised to review my life the *next* day if I wasn't drunk. Still I heard Leroy's voice, *"I remember when you used to give me money."*

I got up and went to the pool table. I had put some money down earlier and believed I was well overdue for a game now. It seemed I had arrived right on cue. I played several games and won. How, I don't know. The atmosphere at the table had been jolly and while not fiercely competitive, there was an edge to the games that kept up interest.

As soon as they came in I knew it was trouble, it was written all over their faces. I've seen people like them all my life. Bullies, people who are not happy unless they're making someone else's life hell. They're in every town, every city. They come out of the grass like the snakes they are, with venom within their hearts to cause fear and misery.

They stood around the table leering, watching, scowling. Hey we're here, feel our bad vibes, we are bad men, everybody know that we are here. Look at us. I guess some of the people around the table knew them because soon people disappeared until there were only three of us left with the three of them. I won the game I was playing, but the next guy who had his money down was just about to put his money in the machine when the apparent leader of these snakes said, "I'm next, it's my turn." And the way he said it didn't book any argument; he was saying if you want violence, you just try and play next.

All of a sudden there was this cloud hanging over the table. I looked up and quietly said, 'Please God, not today.' But God must have either been asleep or declaring, "You will be tested today my boy." The guy whose game it was, gave up the cue and tried to style it out by saying, "I'm just gonna get a drink." One of the leader's henchmen said, "Don't fucking come back, fool." Now the guy he said that to wasn't a small guy, and this looked like it wasn't going to be to good for me.

I was on my own. Everybody had gone and I was left with these three pieces of shit. As I looked around I could see the other patrons peeping from the other side of the bar as if they were waiting for some horrific show to begin, like a car crash they didn't want to stop and stare at but were fascinated by. I looked at these three guys and began to sober up because I knew from people's reactions that it was 'on top' for someone. I wish I could have put the cue down and gone about my business but the cue was somehow stuck to my fingers and was not taking kindly to being released. And the more I tried to shake it off, the more it clung to me, whether in fear or just taking the micky I don't know. I don't consider myself a brave person, but like most, I will stick up for my rights.

These three guys were looking at me now as if to say, "Oh, you're a bad man, you don't want to leave the table to us."

"Honest," I really wanted to say to them, "honest you can have the table, I don't want to play anymore really." But nothing would come out. I wanted to say, "If only the cue would leave my hand and fuck off I would gladly leave the table to you." I wanted to say, "I want no trouble, I'm here drowning my sorrows. Leroy said," *I used to give him money. I'm on that tip. I'm trying to get in touch with my inner self. I'm trying to visualise getting myself back together can you not understand this.' Because these snakes had such a hold for so long, it must have seemed to the inhabitants that these people would never be ousted and that the status quo would remain for a long time to come. Because the the inhabitants had given up. And so along came the outsider ME.*

But as I looked at this bunch of thugs it was just as well I kept my mouth shut because they would construe it as a weakness and believe even more that I was afraid of them, which wasn't strictly true. I was more afraid of myself, of what I could do when people disturbed my peace and felt that they could bully me and get away with it. And *Madness*, who must have been sleeping, suddenly came alive. Popping his head up he said, "*What the fuck is going on here. Who do they think they are?*"

It's because of people like these, the world is the way it is. People bullying others and taking what they have and frightening people out of their own homes. I hate bullies— fuck 'em.

"You ready to play mate?"

I looked around to see who had spoken. But it was me. Foolish, foolhardy me. Suicidal, kamikaze me. How I hated *Madness* at times like these, with his air of righteousness. With his bold indignant stance against what he deemed as injustice. But why drag me along with him? Why, oh why oh why, why drag me along?

"You think your gonna win the game?" challenged the gang leader.

I knew then that the only possible way of avoiding trouble was either to throw the game or hope that he was better than me and would win on his own merit. I knew that if I won that game there undoubtedly would be some form of confrontation. The look in his eyes, his whole body language and that of his boys, let me know in no uncertain terms that this was a challenge, a challenge of masculinity, a challenge of authority, a challenge of territory. I, a male bull, was still on his turf and he and his boys wouldn't have that.

I felt the support of those on the periphery. They wanted the bad man to go down, they wanted their space back. This is what they had been waiting for— an outsider to come in and do the deed, an outsider to come and show them how it was done.

FOUR

The game kicked off. Boom! The reds and yellows dashed and raced all around the green baize table looking for shelter, looking for refuge. Looking for, clawing for, one of the pockets - any of the pockets - to sink into and hide from the merciless assault.

One red, one yellow down; they had found safety. My choice. Reds. Blam! Balls scattered everywhere but nothing went down. His turn. He walked to the top of the table and looked at me with a sardonic grin, all the while chalking his cue as he did so. Our first real meaningful eye contact. He obviously thought he had the upper hand; that staring bullshit. Myself, I try and avoid that kind of confrontation. Because if you're serious you don't play that crap, you just do it. Boom!

I looked at the table and began to study it. To my surprise, I had left a very easy yellow to the top left hand corner pocket– easy pot. Though I had never seen this guy play before there was no way he could miss that surely. Yes, he did pot it, but he fluked it. And you should have seen the way he began to carry on.

"You can't play this game ya, you know about this game, you a fool if you think you can win me."

There's nothing I hate and detest more than embarrassment. I've never been able to accept it, I don't think I ever will. By now my face was burning and I was raging inside. And still he kept on, as he fluked another yellow. I had sussed the guy out, he couldn't fucking play. He'd struggle to beat someone less than average in any pub after a few drinks, but I could play.

"Lets play for drinks," I said.

He was just about to take his shot, *Madness* had obviously had enough.

"That's if you want to, if not it's okay."

The geezer nearly choked as he spluttered, "I want a double whiskey when I win," and then promptly missed a shot that any five-year-old would feel confident of potting. The man was stinking out the place.

And then *Madness* took off on a trip all of his own. "Unlucky brother," said a beaming *Madness* who was beginning to warm to the task, "Better luck next time." It even brought a smile to my lips as I looked at the bully and grinned. I was joining *Madness*.

"You think you're a comedian," said the henchman who'd earlier warned off the other pool player. He had his arms not quite folded over his chest in gangster style.

"We'll see, we'll see," he said.

And *Madness* loved it, oh how *Madness* loved it. *"We'll see, will she, will he, will we, hee-hee anyone for tea?"* *Madness* was kicking off and I laughed, because *Madness* was my friend. I laughed because we were both mad.

The pot was boiling nicely, ready to explode. The three weren't so sure anymore, because they now understood that I could be capable of street violence. They realised their miscalculation; it wasn't fear that had held me back. Suddenly it dawned on them; this guy is a nutter and he could be tooled up. I watched their body language. A new respect shone in their eyes. They were still three, but they understood that if they made a wrong move the man in front of them was capable of taking one or all of their lives.

Bang! Right top corner. Crash! Top left corner. Delicate touch, cut into centre pocket. Slam dunk the last red, bottom left corner. Game done.

"I'll have a Southern Comfort, please," I said casually. I didn't want it to go over the top, I didn't want any trouble (but I hated bullies). Besides I didn't call it on.

He didn't look at me, he didn't say a word, he just put the drink on the table and went back to playing pool; only God knows why because he couldn't play to save his life. But then again, he needed the practice.

Some of the patrons who had been hiding now miraculously appeared; clapping, hanging about and shouting out, "Good game!" much to the vexation of the bully and his henchmen. People started coming out of the woodwork, claiming they were next, but the bully had begun playing pool with one of his friends.

The rage I felt earlier was tempered by the tot of Southern Comfort that was placed beside me on the table. But for every moment, for every second after that game, I kept my eye on all three snakes and knew exactly where they were. Even if I didn't seem to be watching them, I was.

I was now seated back at the table I was at when I first came into the pub. I didn't know why.

What on earth possessed me to remain in that pub? The smart thing would have been for me to get out and not look back. Just be glad that no trouble had occurred. But as so often happens when drink is involved, my judgement became somewhat cloudy. I had made the mistake of believing that the situation had been contained. I hadn't stayed to prove anything or put two fingers up to them, it's just that I had become complacent. And with each passing minute, complacency spread, even to *Madness*, who had disappeared to whence he had come thinking it was all over.

My thoughts returned to the state of my life and how I came to be stuck in limbo like this. Not seeming to be going anywhere, standing still, marking time with no foreseeable future and to cap it all, having to face old friends who remembered me back-in-the-day when I was respected.

I saw them approach from the corner of my eye, but late. They stood around the table looking at me. My line of exit wasn't cut off so at least they hadn't come to surround and trap me. I had no weapon, but then the thought came to me that perhaps I should put my hand in my pocket, as though I did have one. Quickly, I dismissed the idea as highly dangerous. If they had theirs and really believed me to have mine, experience had taught me that this would only induce them to use theirs immediately. Self preservation– get yours in first before the other guy.

I kept my right hand where it was, slightly hidden by the table, and used my left hand to drink. As I would, those who are serious before conflict would note such a move. It would signal that the person was ready for whatever was to come, that he was on the ball, aware. But most of all, it said that you were dealing with someone who was used to conflict, someone who had been here before, someone who knew what they were doing.

"Want to play another game?"

"No, thanks."

"You were lucky to win the game," the bully said. He was eyeing me up, looking for weakness–poking, prodding, feeling, pulling; trying to dissect what was before him.

I spoke with a strong cockney accent, but I was black and happy with that fact. I carried myself proud and yet my attire, my dress sense, seemed to be at odds with who I appeared to be. All in all, I was a contradiction to the stereotypes. You could see that I'd been there, done it; though unlike many others, it wasn't something broadcasted loudly. But make no mistake, it was there. You could miss it if you were not careful. They had nearly missed it, but had come back to have another look at the enigma.

"Ah come on, lets play again, you know I can beat you."

"For the second time, no. Thank you very much, thanks for the offer but if you don't mind I'd rather be on my own."

But it seemed this was the weakness they had been waiting for. What, with 'thank you very much,' 'thank you for the offer,' 'if you don't mind.' Words such as these obviously constituted weakness to these men.

"Fuck you," said the first henchman.

"Yeah fuck you," second henchman said.

"You think your something special," the bully interjected.

Violence was in the air. It was on top. Properly on top.

I'm like many people, I don't want trouble, I try and avoid it; maybe I could even be considered a coward. But fear makes you react to things in ways that can even surprise yourself at times.

I'm not the world's best fighter and there were three of them. Maybe one of my pals could take on all three because my pals could have proper rows. But if I've got something in my hand then you're in trouble. If I'd had a tool, I would have dealt with them in such a way that I would feel no sorrow for them afterwards.

"Georgie Porgie pudding and pie, kissed the girls and made them cry. When the boys came out to play, Georgie Porgie ran away!" screamed *Madness* at the top of his

voice as they moved around the table to grab hold of me. They froze momentarily as the scream filled the place, but in the blink of an eye they recovered and reached to grab hold of me. Up in the air went the table. Crash!!! One of the clowns was so shocked that he fell over backwards without even having been touched. I jumped to my feet.

Bang! I got a punch to the side of my head. I grabbed one of them around the waist, and ran him at pace straight into the edge of the bar counter. Splatter! A bottle just missed my head as the bully brought it down on my shoulder. Thud! A kick in the back. Which must have come from the clown who fell over. I knew I had to keep on my feet, I couldn't go down or I would be finished. I got on my toes. Oh, all right then, I got on my bike. And I peddled all around that fucking pub, round the tables just trying to keep out of harms way. Had it been a boxing match the commentator would have said, "Why doesn't he stand and fight, why's he running away all over the place?"

Eventually, I had to drop the bike. And I'll tell you what, I was up on my toes dancing all around that pub like Fred Astaire, and there was no need to bring on the dancing girls I was doing enough dancing for everybody. At one stage they nearly cornered me, but I danced my way out of that. A few bottles and glasses were on target but I somehow managed to dance them off.

There seemed to be several people trying to break it up now. But I couldn't be sure who was friend and who was foe; this wasn't my area so I didn't know the people or the faces. Then...Yeah, you guessed it I slipped! I banged my head and was nearly out cold and just missed getting my face hit with a bottle. How I moved my head in time, I don't know. Where I got the strength from I can't say, but the bottle missed me by a whisker. All of the sudden, miraculously, it was over. People had parted us. It's like these guys had proven something and it was now all over.

I watched their body language across the room. Laughing and joking like it was all a bloody game; now we could all go about our normal business as if nothing had happened. I thought, your having a laugh but this isn't finished, this has just begun. You think you can bully me and get away with it? You're having a laugh.

The police came mob-handed through the door. But after talking to the landlord they left. I say they left, but a patrol car sat opposite the pub just watching.

The three went back to the pool area and carried on as if nothing had happened; my head was still spinning. There was no doubt in my mind whatsoever, I was going to do the bully. And I thought, you stupid fools you don't know what you've done or let yourself in for. You think it's over, forgotten, but it never will be until I've done you.

As I walked towards them on my way out of the pub, the bully spat across the table just missing my face and hitting my shoulder. I smiled and carried on walking. If I didn't know it before, I knew it now. I was going to kill him. I don't mean I was going to stab, cut him or any other such thing, I was going to end his life—forever. I WAS GOING TO KILL HIM.

I OPENED MY EYES and took a deep breath of the crisp, fresh, night air. It was still October and I was still on the park bench by the small man-made pond, and I had been thinking how it all began. I became aware of the heavy thing in my overcoat pocket. It was time to go, but I would be back: to hunt, seek, find, and in the end, destroy. As I made my way back to Finsbury Park station, I couldn't but help thinking about where all this was leading. And once again, as it had throughout my life, arose the question of what was to become of me. The pocket of my overcoat weighed heavy against my leg as I wiped a tear from my eye.

Wether it was from the cold, I'm not sure. As I headed off into the cold night, I again thought back to my childhood.

FIVE

In 1969 after leaving the welfare building in Holland park with Mr Logey, we went to his house. He lived in Hampstead, not far from the station. His house was very nice. It had a freshness and openness about it that made me feel happy. And more importantly, I didn't feel uncomfortable and nor it seemed did he. We got on very well. And looking back, I can see now that he was glad of my company. He was light-hearted and bubbly with a kindness that I will never forget.

One day a few of Mr Logey's friends came round and one of the ladies inquired, "Who's the young boy, Bill?" Mr Logey explained that the woman who called herself my mother had abandoned me and gone off to America. The woman was incredulous. I could hear and feel her sorrow at my plight and the kindness in her voice when she spoke.

They did not know that I had overheard their conversation; I had been outside the door about to enter. Instead, I headed for the kitchen. I felt ashamed, as if I was a burden placed upon other people. Not really wanted, but tolerated and pitied.

That night, I took my hold-all filled with my possessions and walked out into the night. I couldn't tell you where I was headed or what I was going to do. And after hours of walking I couldn't tell you where I was. I got on an underground train and decided to go to the West End where I had been a few times before. There were bright lights, lots going on, kids my age roaming about and it seemed that in the West End people never slept.

The train pulled into Piccadilly Station. As I got off the train I felt tired and hungry. I checked in my pocket. I had nine quid. I wish I could have gone back to Mr Logey's but I couldn't, too much shame. I promised to give him a call to let him know I was all right. Outside the station was a hive of activity. It was a new world to me– vibrant and alive; somewhere to hide my shame.

Still fresh in my mind were images of Mr Logey's lady friend who spent the afternoon smothering me with kisses and telling me how wonderful I was. I believe she felt terribly guilty at the situation I was in. Why on earth she should, I do not know. But as I have throughout my life, I avoided or ran away from those who cared for me - the coward that I am - afraid to face what I wanted most, love.

I disappeared into the Piccadilly crowd lost in my own world. It was 7:30 p.m.

The night I left Mr Logey's house for the West End was something of an anti-climax. After an hour there I made my way back to the comfort of his home.

For a 15-year-old Catholic boy who lived most of his life in convents and children's homes, the West End soon turned out to be too much of a decadent world.

After staying at Mr Logey's I was soon moved on to another place in Oakley Street in Chelsea. That was a house situation with two women staff members but it was only temporary.

I was soon moved to a hostel; just off the Harrow Road in west London. I hated the place. I was aged 16 and the youngest person there. Full of the dregs of society, I loathed being there and wished I could have gotten out. But I had nowhere else to go.

I soon found out what racism was about and how people took liberties with others if they were allowed to. Even though I was the youngest there, I wasn't about to let anyone take liberties with me. Most of the people in that hostel had been in jail or such.

I don't think the authorities were prepared for people like me back in those days. I was brought up a Roman Catholic. I served mass and benediction and went to a Catholic school. I had an almost middle class upbringing. What was I doing here? I didn't even want to be in London.

One evening I was asked by a couple of the guys at the hostel if I wanted to go to a club in nearby Paddington. I was really bored so I said 'yes'. One was white, the other black and aged 19 and 20 they seemed much older than me who was 16 at the time.

I should say by this time at the hostel, I had managed to get an apprenticeship as an electrician and was attending college one day a week.

The Crypt club turned out to be wonderfully lively and made my first taste of a club a memorable experience. But later on that evening the memories were to become unpleasant ones.

The Crypt was a youth club, run by a really nice vicar and his wife. It was what you'd call a black club I guess. They played reggae and soul music and most of the guys there were black. The women in contrast were mainly white and I remember thinking that it seemed odd.

I was brought up in a white environment surrounded by white people but I was fascinated by my own but had never really spoken to a black girl before. The few that were in the club that night, I watched in awe and amazement. As they danced and laughed I was fascinated.

As a 16-year-old Catholic boy, I'm sure I stood out that night. Many times people would say, "where you come from?" If you couldn't see my face and just heard my accent I'm sure people would have said I was white. Nearly all the guys at the club had some sort of West Indian accent, mainly a Jamaican one. Also to my astonishment so did the few white guys there. Even the bloke I'd come with from the hostel, had miraculously acquired one.

Soon it was time to leave the club but not before a girl had given me her phone number. 'Hoo-bloody-ray'! At last I would have a girlfriend! Well hopefully.

I felt on cloud nine. At last I was feeling like I fitted

in. I had a job I liked and from where I was coming from, felt like I had a lot of money.

Yeah, I felt on top of the world as I walked down Porchester Road with the other two. We were talking amongst ourselves minding our own business when a bloke who was obviously very drunk bumped into Ralph, the white guy I was with from the hostel.

The drunk started to get very aggressive and abusive and before you knew it a little scuffle had broken out between him and Ralph. The black guy went to break them up but was greeted by a punch to the mouth from the drunk who obviously thought he was heavyweight champ of the world.

Well it was all up in the air now but still more like a school playground fight. The two guys didn't want to hurt the drunk and were more pushing him around than laying into him. Yet the drunk is screaming and shouting the odds. Then all of a sudden he starts to shout that they are trying to rob him, which of course they weren't. These two guys then started to leg it and they were calling for me to run off with them.

While all this had been going on I had been standing about 15 to 20 feet away not involving myself in it. I stood there not knowing what to do. Deep down I was kind of frightened about what was taking place. I was a 16-year-old raised in the genteel world of Catholic homes. I wasn't prepared for things like this.

I decided I wasn't running anywhere as I had done nothing wrong. I had time to walk off but I was so bemused by the situation that I didn't know what to do. I couldn't understand why they had run off when they had done nothing wrong. It was all the drunk's fault.

The man was still screaming, "they tried to rob me" as the police car pulled up. As the cops ran up to him he pointed in my direction and shouted, "he's one of them, he's one of them".

Still rooted to the spot in a state of shock, the police rushed me and even though I offered no resistance they jumped onto me, choked me and nearly broke my arm. As they were putting me inside the car they deliberately hanged my head against the door frame several times. I couldn't even speak, as I was in a state of shock. As the police car sped into the night, all I could think of, was what was going to happen to me.

BACK TO THE PRESENT AND I'm on the journey back to Stockwell, I could not help but replay my meeting with Leroy– over and over and over again. *I remember when you used to give me money, Trevor.* Thankfully my thoughts were interrupted when the train stopped at Victoria and two smart black guys sat opposite me, each accompanied by a wonderful black woman. The two women gave me that quick, one-second glance that sizes up everything and can without a second look, determine whether you have any potential. The guys were friendly and nodded in my direction, I acknowledged them with a raise of my eyebrows.

It came to me, as I sat opposite the couples, that there was something missing from my life. First thing I needed was new clothes; I couldn't remember the last time I bought some. The train stopped at Vauxhall; the two guys and girls had arrived at their stop. As one of the girls got up, she looked straight at me and smiled. It was an open, fresh smile and in full view of the guy I assumed to be her boyfriend. He had no worries, he was confident within himself and you could see he seemed to have faith and trust in the lady. For the first time in as long as I can remember, my heart skipped a beat and I looked at that woman and I wanted her. I wanted to lie down in bed with her snuggled up and tell her all my problems and secrets. I wanted to hold her close and to tell her I needed love but was afraid of love because I didn't understand love and knew only that love hurt.

As she disappeared from view, I stood up in anticipation of my own stop. As I did so, my pocket felt heavy and my mind flashed back to the bully. But I let it pass quickly because it was only a matter of time before I caught up with him. When I got home I lay down on my bed with a thousand thoughts running through my mind. My life was practically in ruins, I had nothing and was going nowhere. From being one of the boys, I had let myself go on a downward spiral; a slippery slope that led right to the doo-doo.

Doo-doo land is another zone. A zone where reality separates from society. And in that zone you don't care for yourself, never mind others. The zone is lawless; the rules simple: you survive the best you can. There's no moralistic code, there's no undying friendships and there's no room for love of your fellow human being. Violence, skulduggery, murder, prostitution and drugs are the order of the day. And when you are on drugs as I had been - believe this, if you believe nothing else - it's hard to come back.

With so many thoughts running through my head it was a while before I could get to sleep. Before I finally drifted off, I promise myself to get my life on track. People who thought I was finished didn't know me. I've got a heart of a lion and I'll never give up. Never. I wrote out Frank's number and left it on the dressing table.

I dreamt of wonderful things, happy things, and the suffering of many years past seemed to dissolve. People smiled, laughed and were kind and good to one another. Then a voice from somewhere in my dream shouted, *"Don't do it Trevor. Forgiveness is everything, forgive and forget!"*

All of a sudden I appeared in a large crowd. I stood on a chair and screamed, *"Why should I forgive? Liberties have been taken. Why should I forgive? You know my life's not like that."* At the sound of my voice the crowd panicked and dispersed in all directions. And for the first time I realised they were all wearing white gowns. The voice came back, *"Your whole life has been unforgiving, unloving, unyielding, uncompromising. And may I add unproductive!!"*

I still could not see the person belonging to the voice. The crowd had disappeared. It was as if I had broken up a wonderful, happy party. *"You told me an eye for an eye, a tooth for a tooth. You've got that written down,"* I continued to shout blindly, still standing on my chair. Suddenly it went dark and I seemed to be falling, falling, falling. Then I heard, *"I also said vengeance is Mine."*

I opened my eyes to a shaft of sunlight peeking through the chink in the curtain onto my face. It felt warm and nice. I sighed deeply and smiled. I stretched, curled into a ball and stretched again. It felt good. I felt as if I was alive and ready to live again; ready to join the human race. And maybe, after many years of being alone, I would find myself a nice girl. Today somehow seemed to re-release my spirit and it felt good. I didn't want to analyse it, I just wanted to go with the flow. I looked across the dresser and saw the white piece of paper with Frank's phone number on it. I smiled, and jumped out of bed.

Frank owned a car front across the tracks in north London. Quite a large car front in fact; quite nice, with expensive and at times exotic cars. I had a lot of time for Frank and the relationship and mutual respect we had for each other taught me that not all white people were bad.

I first met Frank in prison back in the day; on the island in maximum security. There had been a stand-off on the landing one tea time. It was over some black issue. But as the guards - the screws - started to appear, most black guys ran into their cells and closed the doors. A few of us stayed to front it out with them. Then all of a sudden this stocky, short, white guy comes up the stairs. Comes and stands with the five of us left, looks at the screws and says, "I'll have some of this an' all, Governor." Anyway, thank God it never kicked off. But Frank and myself were friends from that day onwards.

I arrived in north London around 11:30 a.m. It was a

cold, grey day with an icy wind that seemed to reach deep into my bones, leaving my ears tingling and the tips of my fingers freezing even though I had gloves on. The sun shone high in the sky. *Why was it so damned cold?* I turned the corner into the road where Frank's car lot was, but it wasn't there. Stunned, I just stood and stared at the tall redbrick building that stood in the place where Frank's car front used to be.

The building it turned out, was an office block fronting for some overseas foreign corporation. I made enquiries at the desk but nobody seemed able to give me any information. As I stepped out of the building with the intention of asking one of the shop owners, someone shouted, "Oh mate, hold up!" I turned to see an old boy in a security uniform coming out of the building. He hadn't run far, yet he was panting for breath like he'd just run the 100 metres.

"Take it easy mate. You'll have an heart attack," I said to him. He looked up and smiled at me. "Na, na, mate I'm aright. It's just I came back from the bog, and they told me you were looking for the people who used to be here before. That was Frank's car place, is that correct?"

"Yeah, that's right mate."

"Well they've moved to Gordon Road; it's about a mile up the there."

"Is it still a large car front?"

"Oh Yeah," said the old boy nodding his head. It looked like he loved giving out information to people. I guess his job must have been pretty boring. It just felt like he was happy to talk to someone, anyone.

"He's gone a bit up-market now. Well, since his

wife's died, I don't suppose he's got any need to save money now. Is he a friend of yours?"

"How long ago did his wife die?"

"About three years now. I even went to the funeral. I only live three blocks away. I lived in this area all my life . . . ."

I didn't hear the rest, all I knew was that Lyn was dead. Poor Frank must be devastated. He loved that woman so much. Lyn was wonderful to me, had even put me up when I was on the run several years ago. I couldn't believe it had been three years since I last saw Frank and Lyn. But when I looked back, it had been at least five years.

I had Frank's home phone number and I knew where he lived. I could quite easily have gone round his house. But because I hadn't seen him in so long, I thought I'd drop in, then let him invite me back to his home at the end of day after we'd gone for a drink.

Lyn was dead. Phew! That was a blow, she was a lovely girl.

"Are you listening mate?"

The security man was in front of me, with his arm outstretched pointing into the distance.

"As I was saying, it's about a mile in that direction. Keep right and bear to the right and keep going. You can't miss it, Gordon Road. And with that he was off, climbing the stairs back to his official job. I headed off in the direction he had pointed, still trying to comprehend what I had been told.

THE YEARS 1975-1982 I SPENT in the boob– seven years

for armed robbery and did two years in solitary confinement. A year of that was for my involvement in the Gartree riots in Leicester's maximum security prison.

After serving the seven years, I wrote and had published, a book entitled *Labelled A Black Villain.* It was then that I teamed up with Frank and several others. I trusted Frank with my life. And I remember when he first met Lyn; I can remember it like it was yesterday. They were so in love, believe me.

We had just done a bit of work and we were all flush. We all lived our own separate lives of course, but came together for bits of work. Though we didn't see each other every day, we had a bond that was tight.

That Saturday night we decided to go out to celebrate and ended up in some mixed club. Black and white people dancing, raving together, having a grand time in the West End. We had lots of dough, and to see us you would know we were on a high. We got well and truly plastered, but throughout the night Frank kept disappearing onto the dance floor with some girl. Nobody paid much attention because we were all out of it. Smashed. And besides, we all at some stage disappeared onto the dance floor with some girl or other.

Time to go and get our cabs. We all bundled out into the street. Six of us had arrived together. Three black guys, three white guys. But now, there were about twelve guys and ten girls. Apparently we had been invited to some party, in Maida Vale, I think.

Anyway we got down there and it turned out to be some nice people we had known a long time. One thing stood out that night. The girl Frank had picked up at the club and brought along, never left his side. Not even when we were bonding at the bar, plotting-up and having a good time.

Frank danced only with her. And when they weren't dancing they would be in some corner spot, kissing and cuddling. Frank got teased mercilessly and ribbed continuously. But he didn't care. We all knew he had found someone special. Her name was Lyn. She was about 5'1", petite, slim, had jet black hair and looked like an elf. But she had wonderful, honest eyes. And that was one thing we all remarked upon.

From that night onwards they were inseparable. And it wasn't long before the rest of us were handed wedding invitations to their marriage. There was only one blip along the way. And that was at the very beginning of their relationship.

There was this old flame of Lyn's who couldn't get it into his head that she had found someone else. He would go round to her work place and cause a scene about how he still loved her and so on. Frank had warned him twice. But seeing that Frank was short and stocky and not as handsome as him - he was about 6' 2" to Frank's 5' 6"- he thought Frank was a mug. And so he started taking the piss.

The thing is, Frank promised Lyn he wouldn't hurt this guy. But one day it got out of hand. Frank went to pick her up and the geezer turned up with two of his pals and started to threaten Frank. Then, he started to threaten Lyn.

A scuffle took place outside her work place. Nothing much, no one got hurt or anything. But had the guy known Frank, he wouldn't have done that. Oh yeah, he said he was going to shoot Frank. Apparently the guy was some Mickey Mouse bouncer on some door. Still, he needed his two buddies to confront Frank. The guy was a coward. Anyway, Frank wasn't having none of it and the guy, unbeknownst to him, was in plenty of trouble.

As we waited in the van in the dark alley, we could see the last of the people leaving the club. The bouncer would soon be on his way to his car, where we would overpower him, put him in the van and take him for a ride he would never forget.

When I got a call from Frank saying he needed a favour, I didn't ask, I just said yes, I'd meet him. Two other pals were there, and he told us what it was all about. The thing is, he'd promised Lyn not to hurt him nor did he want anyone else to hurt him.

"So what we are here for?" someone asked.

"I am going to frighten the fucking life out of him."

We could see the bouncer now walking towards the alley. We were all in the back, doors slightly ajar, at the ready to pounce.

When Frank said he wasn't going to hurt him, that meant that he wasn't going to shoot or stab him and leave him in a pool of blood. Because if this bastard put up too much resistance, we'd beat the granny out of him with the coshes we all now held in our hands.

He approached the alley without a care in the world. But when we jumped out of the van ballied up, he knew it was on top and screamed like a bitch. And he started to fight for his life because I'm sure that's what he believed he was doing. We coshed that motherfucker, threw him in the van, and taped him up like a prize pig.

Thirty seconds later we were driving to our destination. Throughout the drive not one word was spoken. Three of us sat in the back with the prisoner. I knew where we were taking him and what we were about to do and it scared me.

After half an hour's drive, we pulled into the leafy lane off the main road and stopped. We jumped out, grabbed hold of him and proceeded to carry him through the trees further and deeper into the woodlands.

It was about twelve o'clock on a moonlit night. The guy was fully trussed up with white masking tape. As we carried him, he squirmed and wriggled and was now squealing like a stuck pig as he glimpsed one the guys carrying the shovels. When I did manage to glimpse his eyes they reflected sheer terror. Panic.

We dropped him at the pre-arranged spot, and began to dig in silence. I noticed that Frank was still carrying a blue bag that I had seen him with when we had all met up. I asked him what was in it. He just said, "Wait and see, it's a surprise."

The digging had sent our guest into a frenzy and he was flapping about like a fish out of water. And may I say like a very big fish. It didn't take us long to dig a hole that would be big enough to put him, as we'd chosen the place carefully for its soft, easy to remove dirt.

I was all for stopping this now, nipping it in the bud, because it looked like this guy might have a heart attack. Then I thought–fuck him, you don't tell people you're gonna shoot them and bully people you think are mugs, because they're smaller than you. Fuck him. Anyway, the plan was to put him in the hole, start throwing dirt in, then drag him out; mark his card and leave it at that. But as we were putting him down in the hole, Frank said, "Take his trousers off; I want to fuck him first." Well you should have seen the guy's face, I'm telling you.

We all still had our balaclavas on but when I turned round to face Frank, he had a black wet suit on, flippers and all. Oh yeah! And he had a hole in the crotch where his dick was hanging out. I couldn't help it, I had to speak.

"A wat de bloodclaat is dis dred?"

Frank stood in front of me and mouthed, "I'm only joking, I'm only joking."

I managed to give the other two guys the sign that Frank wasn't serious. But they were gob smacked and on the verge of jacking it all in. Then to my amazement, Frank started pulling on his plonker saying, "Get him ready for me, get his trousers off. I wanna give him one before we bury him. Grease him up."

All the while Frank was pulling on his dick, making these loud groaning and moaning sounds and twisting his head from side to side like he was in sheer ecstasy and pleasure. He portrayed the role of a pervert to a tee. I've never seen such fear on a man's face as I did that night.

The outcome was he never went near Lyn again. And by all accounts he had moved out of the area. As far as I knew, Frank never saw him again. The guy knew it was Frank, but by then people had marked his card. And I will tell you, don't play about with a man who's deeply in love. When it concerns his woman, men become irrational. And there's always a chance there may be fireworks.

There it was in front of me– Frank's Place.

SIX

Frank's Place was on the corner of a busy junction and was quite a fair size. On the forecourt the cars gleamed and sparkled as a number of men and boys busied themselves at various tasks. All in all, it looked like a very nice set-up, like the man was doing very nicely for himself.

I headed straight for the office, it looked rather plush and comfortable. As I entered and took two steps inside, I was confronted by a large African Ridgeback dog which stood in front of me, head cocked to one side with a quizzical look.

A tall fellow with a bald head stood a few feet away leaning against the door frame leading into an inner office. There was a grin on his face that dared me to take a step closer. I took a step forward and knelt down.

"Hello girl, good girl, come on," I said in a soft voice,

all the while looking at the dog as it stepped forward for me to rub its head.

"Good girl, who's a good girl?"

The dog licked my hand. The tall fellow wasn't smiling anymore.

"Trevor, Trevor, you bastard." Frank came out and was bear-hugging me, dancing with me, saying repeatedly, "You bastard," through a very wide smile. I had forgotten how short Frank was. But now that he had added several pounds to his frame - mainly to his stomach and behind - he now looked even shorter than I remembered. But there was no disguising that Frank grin, I knew it had to be a proper pal.

"Keith told me, 'There's some black geezer looking and he's about to come in. Doesn't look like he's got two pennies to rub together. The dog will take care of him.' But when the door opened and the dog never barked, I thought, that's strange!" Frank turned to Keith and said, "He's not like most black men, he loves dogs and dogs love him. And he loves doing that to people's dogs. Especially when they think he should be frightened of them. He gets a buzz out of it. What he usually says is, 'Where I come from we've got lions!'"

Frank was still hugging and pulling me in his happiness to see me. I wasn't quite sure about the dog now which was standing and looking at me while growling deep down in its chest.

"Sit down, Caber!" Frank shouted. The dog immediately sat down, still looking at me.

We went into the plush inner office and seated

ourselves at a lovely green leather-topped table. On seeing Frank's greeting towards me, Keith offered an apology.

"No disrespect mate, there's a lot of crack heads and people trying to sell things around here, so can't be too careful."

I took an instant dislike to him.

"That's all right mate," I said. What do crack heads look like? Black?"

Frank pinched me discreetly and winked.

"I never meant nothin' by it, mate."

"It's all right bruv, I'm only joking."

Frank formally introduced us. And it just goes to show, you can't judge a book by it's cover; Keith turned out to be a very nice guy.

Frank left Keith in charge and threw him a bunch of keys as we both walked out of the door. He gave me a tour of the car lot. I must confess, while doing the rounds I thought, *He's doing nicely, surely he'll give me a nice motor if I ask him.* I was skint and embarrassed. I had a tenner to my name and that was it. I had already noticed Frank taking inventory of my attire. And I'm sure he knew I was bang in trouble. News always seems to get around and bad news even quicker. Even though we had only been talking superficially, I'm sure Frank would have heard about my troubles. About my wife leaving and taking my 3-month-old son to Ghana without my knowledge, about my substance abuse and general tumble down the ladder. I'm not sure how *much* he knew, but seeing me here in front of him, he couldn't fail to understand that this wasn't the same Trevor.

We were friends, but friends can become liabilities. If you weren't on the ball, you could jeopardise other people's freedom, i.e. loose tongue, not being as careful as you should be, talking to the wrong person, mixing with the wrong company, not having your wits about you, not seeing what was coming before it comes. But what I feared most of all was the loss of respect.

As the day wore on, I knew that Frank hadn't lost respect for me, because that's something that's very hard to conceal.

"Come on son, were off now," Frank said as he opened the driver's door to a top of the range Mercedes. He got in; I opened the passenger side door and slid in beside him.

"Where's your motor?"

"I haven't got one mate, that's how down I've been."

Frank looked across at me, smiled and said, "You have now, we'll pick you out one when we get back." With that, he slipped a Bob Marley CD in the player, pulled out smoothly and joined the busy flow of traffic as Bob sang, "...we're jamming, we're jamming in the name of the Lord..."

With a big grin on my face, I turned to Bob and yelled, "Praise the Lord!"

I CANNOT AND will never speak badly of my wife, my son's mother; nor will I allow others to. Let the record show that I am to blame. The other party is blameless until such time in which the wages of our sins are weighed.

The years of being in children's homes without a family was hard for me as I'm sure it was for the others. And many nights I laid down and cried in my bed, vowing that if I had children I would never ever let anything like this happen to them. When I grew up I would get married and it would be forever and ever; as a Roman Catholic there *is* no divorce. I would talk to my child, play with my child, laugh and cuddle my child, but most of all I would love my child.

As Frank drove, we both sat back to listen to the music. I again began to think about my childhood and the evil McCann.

In the dining hall standing behind our chairs, waiting for the father to say grace, Mr McCann came up behind me and said, "You're talking Hercules." Everybody was talking, we always did, but in low voices. It was just an excuse for McCann to come and bully a victim for the day. He stood behind me, put one hand either side of my ears, spread his arms wide and then brought them together with such force on my ears that I thought that my head would explode. He did this twice, then calmly walked off.

It was a while before I heard Stewie Gargan, who was head of our table and two years older whisper, "Don't cry, don't cry." I took a chance, my life in my hands, and whispered back, "I'm not going to." At that precise moment I hated my mother and whoever my father was for the shame and indignity I had to bear at the hands of this tyrant. This was supposed to be a Catholic home, what type of people were these? Again I vowed I would never leave my child to a fate such as this.

Days earlier we had been cleaning inside the church and one of the priests came up and said to a small boy named Carl Munnings, "You were talking." The boy, no older than nine, was doing nothing. "Watch my right hand, watch my right hand," said the priest as he held his right hand ready to slap the boy. Bam! He slapped him with the left hand."Watch my right hand, watch my right hand. As the boy did so -Bam!- he hit him with the left. And so this went on, even after Carl was rolled up in a ball like a hedgehog, crying for help. But who was there to help him? This was all we knew.

I was working in the pantry; after tea everyone talks. McCann as his want, just appeared from nowhere. It seemed he spent his whole time sneaking up on us. "You're talking Hercules." He drew back his fist and punched me full in the mouth, expecting me to go down. He then half turned to walk away but turned back, surprised I hadn't moved. I looked him straight in the face and said,"You ever put your hands on me again and I will kill you." I was 14 years of age. He was so shocked he just started to back out of the door. But not before I saw the fear in his eyes. He realised I was becoming a young man. And he was no longer sure that he could overpower me if it came to it.

From that day on, he never laid another finger on me. Later myself and Joseph Mclish ran away, but we had nowhere to go. Starving hungry, we came back and were given the cane by Father Ryan, a priest who used to kick people whenever the mood took him. We had supper, then went to bed– a wonderful form of escapism, at least until the morning. Then after that, wonderful, lovely school. Away at least for sometime from the nightmare of the children's home.

I OPENED MY EYES JUST as Frank pulled up outside a pub just off the Old Kent Road. "Come on mate, I've just got to see someone inside."

The pub was like any local boozer at that time in the afternoon. There weren't that many people in there and those who *were* there looked as if that was the way they spent their afternoons. Two well- dressed men stood at the far side of the bar and on recognising Frank, waved him over. Seeing me, they gave Frank a quizzical look. They shook hands and then Frank introduced me as an old, good and loyal friend putting much emphasis on the 'loyal,' which seemed to put the men at ease.

After all the introductions, we found ourselves a quiet table in the corner. Both men were impeccably dressed, and if not for their cockney accents would have been taken as middle class businessmen. I tried to remove myself discretely by saying I was off to play the fruit machine but Frank said, "No, it's all right Trevor, stay where you are mate, it's all right. They then got down to the business at hand, which involved banker's drafts of many thousand of pounds somehow acquired from someone within the bank. Even though the serious matter being discussed was only for private ears, my presence there was acceptable because those men knew I would never have been in Frank's company unless I was completely trusted.

Business finished, we all got up to leave and went our separate ways.

"Hungry?"

"Yeah, I am as it happens."

"I know a nice pie and mash shop down the road," Frank said, as we got in the car.

I love my West Indian and African food but I must admit I do like a pie and mash, regardless of the stick I used to get from some of the black guys. For black guys born here, from back in the day, having a pie and mash was normal. And the event of my pal, Les Fash, taking us all for a pie and mash was well and truly an expression of us being so called "black" English.

During our meal I expressed my sorrow to Frank at the death of his wife Lyn. A sadness came into his eyes that was like looking at a window into his soul. I saw all the hurt and pain and suffering that he was still going through even after all this time. We spoke about many things. And yes, he had heard about my marital problems and expressed his deep regret and sorrow at the loss of my son. Of my other problems, he said not a word. If he knew or not, I don't know, but on that subject nothing was forthcoming.

It's difficult to hide things from people who know you, especially if they haven't seen you for a long time; they can see the change in you. To Frank's credit, he was very diplomatic when I gave a brief synopsis of how I had reached this point in my life. I couldn't even tell him that I was doing anything constructive. Though I wanted to lie, I knew he would see through any bullshit, so in the end I just gave it to him straight.

"To tell the truth Frank, for a while I just lost the plot."

"Don't worry mate we all make mistakes, we've all been there. You'll get it together mate, don't worry, you'll get there."

On the drive back to his car lot Frank said, "There's no need for words, I know the coup, I'll give you as much help as I can. But people are talking and you know it's time to get it together and fuck 'em all."

I knew then that he did know about my problem with substance abuse.

We arrived at the car lot just as Keith was locking up. Frank took back the keys from Keith who then got into a Range Rover and after an exchange of goodbyes, drove off. Caber, the Ridgeback, followed me and Frank back into the office where we talked about the old days, who was where and who was doing what. Frank surprised me by explaining that although he looked flush, much of it was just show. He said the other car front he had up the road had financial difficulties after his wife died. He had taken his eye off the ball and had also had a minor breakdown, which was all news to me.

"Nearly all the cars out the front Trevor, are leased. I've got this deal with some company which benefits both of us. But the bottom line is, most of what I had, I've lost. I'm not skint, but a few years ago I decided to go straight. Things haven't worked out, so just recently I've started to do bits and pieces. But don't worry mate, I might not have loads of cash but I can afford to give you a car," he said smiling.

"Thank God for that. After you telling me all that I thought, 'No, he can't do it.'"

"I can just about do it Trev, but it will be and old Ford Fiesta."

My heart sank. Anyway, what did I expect? At least it was a car.

Frank took some keys from a rack on the wall. "How broke are you?"

I looked at him and just shrugged my shoulders. How do you tell a friend you haven't seen in years that you've only got about eight pounds to your name?

Frank bent down and opened a cupboard. Though not concealed, you would hardly have noticed it was there. It turned out to be a medium-sized safe. He took out two very large wads of bank notes and handed them to me.

"There's five grand there Trev, sorry it can't be more at the moment but we'll try and work something out.

"That's okay Frank, that's *more* than okay."

"Shut up. I remember the amount of times you looked after me in the past. Maybe other people might forget but I haven't, you're a good man."

We walked out onto the forecourt and weaved between a row of cars. He stopped at a smart blue Saab and handed me the keys. This certainly wasn't an old Fiesta and I realised Frank had been pulling my leg. As I unlocked the driver's side door and slid in, he came to the near side window, looked at me and winked. He came round, got in beside me and said, "Drive it to the side of the road."

We sat in the car and talked for a while. He was off to some meeting and we arranged to meet up later in the week and hit the town. I put the car smoothly into gear and headed into the rush hour traffic. Smiling from ear to ear I thought, it's been a long time since someone I knew offered me such kindness. Perhaps my luck was changing after all.

I headed over to Ladbroke Grove to see an old friend. And yes, to show off my new car. But as I drove west across London I knew it wouldn't be easy to get myself back together after being down for so long. Again, I contemplated my downfall.

Alone, and without the 3-month-old child I had watched being born, my life meant nothing to me. Whisked away to far off lands, he was beyond my reach. I was alone with my pain and heartache. Had I been a man of a softer, gentler persuasion, less harsh, less dogmatic, more understanding, and of course less stubborn, I'm sure things or at least something would have been able to be worked out.

But at that time I was unforgiving. If you crossed the line, that was it. I didn't want to hear any stories from anybody. What do you mean second chance, you made a mistake. No! I wasn't into that. I lived by a code and the code *I* had. Everyone else must live by it. A liberty was a liberty, there was no going back on that; was there? Wasn't I staunch and those around me? Wasn't I a proper man who lived by a man's code? No grassing, no telling tales, look after your own or mug yourself off. How could a man– what type of man, would run after a woman who had taken his child to foreign lands and tell her that he loved her? I couldn't do that could I; what type of man would I be?

The cold, hard code that I lived by was my undoing. And so with my code I hid away, with my hurt and with my shame. The flat became my prison. I threw out all the reminders of what had once been a family home. Hadn't I tried to do the right thing– gone and got married; no baby father business for me. Yet here I was– alone. No wife and no child.

Under cover of darkness I drove off to places where bright lights, loud music and much alcohol helped dull the senses and helped me forget, for a while at least. And of course I went to places where nobody knew me. I'd always sneak back into my flat, desperate to avoid the neighbours. I even parked my car in a different place so that they wouldn't know that I was in. But you can only hide for so long.

By now, most of my neighbours knew the situation anyway. After all, how could they not? Didn't they see me everyday pushing the pram, showing men how it should be done? Didn't they see me carrying my child to the paper shop everyday and along the way letting him touch everything: bushes, leaves, trees. flowers, even walls; all part of my master plan to make him aware and conscious of the world and his surroundings from the earliest of ages.

I had so much knowledge and wisdom to teach him.

I had been there, seen it, done it. He would have known unequivocally that he could be anything he wanted to be. And, *believe it*, he would have been anything that his heart desired, including Prime Minister. I had that kind of power to give.

For all intents and purposes my life was finished. Because according to my beliefs, once married– that's it. And I could never have another child outside of my marriage. Then one day I got a huge surprise, much to my confusion. Where I lived many of my neighbours were quite elderly and I was always ready to help with their shopping or give a helping hand if they had any problems. One day there was a knock on the door and a delegation of about five elderly ladies, whom I knew very well, presented themselves. Not thinking, I opened the door to them. With much sympathy they came in and despite my protests cleaned my flat, sat me down and had a heart to heart telling, assuring me that things would be all right.

It was one of the most wonderful things that has ever happened to me in my life. And I will never ever forget the kindness of those dear old girls. It made me, for one moment, realise that I wasn't such a bad person.

SEVEN

I pulled up outside my friend's house in Ladbroke Grove. I gave his door several knocks but he wasn't in. Guess I'd have to wait to show off my new shiny blue Saab. I got back into my car and sat there. My head was still spinning with all the thoughts I had had while driving across London and thinking about the beginning of my downfall. It was after seven and it was already dark. I laid my head back against the headrest, closed my eyes, and thought some more....

It was 1987. There was a big hole in my armour. Coming out of the pictures one night in the West End, walking along the brightly-lit crowded streets as people passed me by happy and laughing and I, oh so alone, I knew then and there how and why, people committed suicide.

The shame, the pain and the hurt still continued and

my very good, loyal and trusted friends I avoided at all cost. The times that I did see them with their families - at home with their kids, and me without mine - just hurt too much for me to be around.

Now that I was avoiding all my friends, I began to take up with all different kinds of people, who at best, could only be described as acquaintances. These were people who neither shared the same ideology as me or my friends, nor had the same level of manners and respect. Any time my friends saw me with them, they'd pull me aside and ask what I was doing with them and say, "You're not having it with them for f***'s sake are you? What's the matter with you, get rid of them and let's get out of here." But I'd always make some excuse and slip my friend to make off with my new acquaintances who didn't know about my hurt, pain and shame.

My friends were very protective towards me because they knew I was very vulnerable at that time, and as a 'firm' we guard and look after each other's welfare. But there was nothing they could do. I moved from that lonely flat and hid myself away.

Eventually I took up with a mixed-race guy named Fiss, who I had known in prison. He was an out-and-out nutter who obviously had some deep-rooted problem but never mentioned it. Whether it was a woman or what I don't know, but I was glad of the company because all he seemed to want to do was get out of his nut on booze every night and that suited me fine because it helped me to forget. We went to bars, pubs, clubs, you-name-it; we went and got sloshed and I mean *sloshed*. We'd put our arms around each other's shoulders and do a knees-up while singing drunken football songs at the top of our voices when we wanted it to kick-off. Who egged who on wasn't a consideration because we both had demons inside of us and our eyes were wild. We wanted to be on the edge, in the fast lane.

One chilly December morning, I found myself outside Palmers Green tube station waiting to meet with a friend I hadn't seen for years. He had given someone his phone number and told them to give it to me urgently, as he wanted to speak to me. He hadn't been 'out' long and we had missed each other on two separate occasions.

His name was Don and he was a real ladies' man. You'll understand why when I tell you that he was a dead ringer for Denzil Washington. We clasped hands firmly and smiled; it was good to see him and I knew the feeling was mutual. We drove back to his place, just off Golders Green.

As we climbed the steps of a very conservative maisonette, I smiled, nodded at him and said, "I'm impressed." The inside was tastefully furnished in chintz and as I took in the décor a wonderfully long-legged Nubian-type beauty said, "Hello." This time he looked at *me* and smiled.

The outcome of our meeting was that he had £20,000 worth of jewellery and asked me if I could get rid of it for him; all he wanted was £5,000. The stuff was pucker and I knew someone who would take it straight away, so we went downstairs to the phone box to make the call, though he had a phone in the flat.

The person I rang was very interested and we arranged to meet outside Seven Sisters tube station at seven o'clock that evening. Unfortunately Don couldn't make it at seven o'clock and entrusted me to go on my own. He repeated that anything I got over the £5,000 was mine to keep.

Later on that afternoon I met up with Fiss. He came along with me to Seven Sisters where we met up with Bob, who was an oldish white guy, but had his finger on the pulse. We parked my car, transferred to his Range Rover and drove to his house in Chingford where I had been several times before.

His wife, although well into her fifties, was an attractive blonde with a neat figure and a great sense of humour; I got on very well with her. Bob's relationship with his wife was quite close. You could see that after many years of being together they were tight and he did the business openly in front of her. She was his second pair of eyes and anything he missed, I'm sure she didn't.

All the pieces were laid out on a glass-topped table. Bob fingered them with an expert's touch, every once in a while making guttural sounds to himself, but I knew he liked what he saw.

He asked me my price and I said seven grand. He laughed and said six.

"No, seven, you know it's worth that much; you're getting a bargain, next you'll be asking me to give it to you for nothing!"

"I can't do it, my money's tied up in something else at the minute Trevor, I can't do it mate."

I took my time because I knew he wanted it. His wife, right on cue, began to pour us large brandies. I deliberately changed the subject to something else which included Fiss, to give Bob time to look at the goods on the table and make a better offer. Soon, he disappeared next door. His wife sat down, admiring the pieces. Bob reappeared with a bag of white powder. "I can't do no more Trevor, six grand and one ounce of Charlie, that's my last offer, take it or leave it."

At this point, Fiss jumped in and urged me to take it. I thought, why the f*** had I brought him. I urged Bob to give me £800 instead of the Charlie but he said he couldn't, he didn't have the money and that he would already have to borrow a grand from next door if the deal was to go through. I said, "All right."

From under the very table we were gathered around, he reached and produced five bundles with elastic bands around them. "That's five grand. I'll be a minute, I'm going next door to borrow the other grand." When he came back and settled up, we shook hands and I could see he was quite happy about the deal. On the way out, his wife gave me a bottle of champagne and Fiss a bottle of brandy.

I put both my hands to my head in mock horror and looked at Bob, then his wife. I said, "Oh no, I've been done." But we all laughed. I was happy and I knew he was.

Don was happy with the money I'd brought back and before I left we arranged to meet again and go to a club next Saturday. That suited me fine, because wherever Don went there was always sure to be plenty of girls around.

It was after eleven when Fiss and I left Don's. Throughout the journey back, Fiss was on my case about how he could get rid of the Charlie, which he conveniently had put in his pocket. Just to shut him up, I let him drive. He said he knew a place over in Brixton where we could get rid of the stuff. We had popped open the champagne and I was beginning to get so drunk I didn't care anymore. What was happening? Who was I? Where was I? Who cared?

As the bright lights whizzed past, Fiss gulped down the last of the champagne and swerved the Mercedes.

"Watch out for the police mate," I said to Fiss.

"F*** the police!" said Fiss and I took up the chant, "F*** the police! F*** the police!" and we chanted and sang that song, our favourite song, *F*** the police!* which were in fact, the only words. I opened the bottle of brandy and with every swig we shouted, "F*** the police!" We loved it.

We finally stopped outside some house on Brixton Hill and both staggered out, me still clutching half a bottle of brandy as Fiss knocked on the door. The length of time and the furtive way in which they opened the door told me that this was a crack house and the moment I walked through that door on Brixton Hill can only be described as the beginning of my WORST NIGHTMARE.

BACK TO THE PRESENT in my blue Saab outside my friend's house in Ladbroke Grove. Eight o'clock and still Dennis was not back. I decided not to wait any longer, but to treat myself to a night out. I deserved it after many years of living in limbo, where one day just merged into the next; living in a different zone from the rest of society, a zone where you did as you liked.

Many had died in that zone, and many more would still die. It was a zone with not much hope, a zone where crime, drugs, prostitution, violence and murder were always on the agenda. And the main course, the dish of the day, was how to survive until the next one.

The zone used to be known as opting out, doing your own thing, trying to find yourself. It was always thought of as a bit of a giggle, a bit of a laugh, putting two fingers up to society and your parents, joining with rebellious others until you found what you were looking for. People seeking alternatives, people who felt they just didn't fit in, people who held grudges, people who felt they were discriminated against, people who had been abused, people who couldn't cope, people who had lost the plot, people who were just plain nasty; these were the occupants of the zone.

And then there were the calculators, people who looked at the zone and its vulnerable victims and realised there was profit to be had from them. Profit to be had from those who are confused. Profit to be had from those who didn't really understand what was going on. Profit to be had if they could infiltrate, muddy the waters and inject a virus that was contagious. So along they came, with crack cocaine, heroin, and money on their minds. They spread their virus and turned the zone into the twilight zone. Before long the good, the bad, and the ugly had been infected with this man-made virus.

There are also those who have a different agenda it would appear. Those in the hierarchy who allowed this to happen and though I can't prove it, I am sure instigated this. They have not stopped it, they have not really tried to stop it. But I believe that they could stop it if they so desired, and at any time.

There are those in power who are happy for crack cocaine to rip through the heart of the black community in particular– destroying it. Destroying the lives of men, women and children young and old. Because the drugs are a very effective form of control which has led to the near collapse and breakdown of family values, outside as well as within the home.

White society still has a fear of black males, especially if we don't aspire to be like them, act and talk like them, walk like them, laugh like them, have the same view point as them. White society still has fear and guilt over the black race, due to what was done by their race to the black race.

THE NIGHTCLUB I went to in the West End was called Moonlight. It was a very nice club. The friend and I who went, managed to swag two gorgeous girls. How, I don't know, but we did. We danced the night away and I couldn't remember the last time I was so relaxed. I forgot about all my past problems and thought maybe going straight really *was* the right thing to do.

That night I found myself at her place, in Hendon, just near the station. She had a ten-year-old son, who was staying the weekend with her estranged husband. Her name was Katie, and she reminded me of a young Nina Simone–tall, proud and regal.

Her house was very well furnished, very chic. I immediately felt at home when I spied a large poster of Angela Davis - afro and all - looking down at me from one of her walls. She was a solicitor, a Sagittarius, with a very warm and caring disposition. She was also quite open and honest and I got the feeling she was quite vulnerable, which surprised me, as the term vulnerable could never be applied to any solicitors *I* knew.

She had an open coal fire that spread lovely, velvety warmth right through me. She had placed a wonderfully large and fluffy rug on the floor, which we now sat on. We sat facing each other with glasses of red wine and were engulfed by the red glow of the fire. The conversation was articulate and sensual; we looked into each other's eyes a lot and smiled.

"Have you ever been in love before Trevor?"

"Don't go there baby."

"Come on, Trev."

"Trev is it now? Why do woman like to probe so soon, its quite disconcerting for men you know."

"Yes I know, I've got a squirmer meter. I always ask that question of men I like. Just to see how much they squirm. It tells me a lot about them."

"So you like me then, that's interesting," said I smiling.

"You've got potential."

"Have I?"

"Yes you have, but you hold back. Somehow I get the feeling you're capable of a deep and tender love."

I felt warm inside, and the wine had made me deliciously light- headed.

HOW AND WHEN it happened, I can't really recall. But we were now holding hands and it seemed the most natural thing in the world to be doing. We weren't self-conscious about it. I guess we both needed someone to empathise with. We spoke about our insecurities and our need for love and hugs. Then we both came together and began hugging each other. The stereo system was playing Horace Andy and Tappa Zukie.

Natty dread a wha' the young girl want.

Yagga, yagga, yagga, ya.

We explored each other riding a surfboard on a wave. The wave started off very small and grew and grew to gigantic proportions.

Her breasts were firm and long nippled and tasted of ooh, aah. I rubbed and gently squeezed and caressed them. I turned her body over, pulled it to me, pushed it away and pulled it back again. I held her ankles and opened her up wide, as she twisted and turned. She sucked on my nipples and I'm sure I cried out in ecstasy. She was doing something to me now that, "Oh good God!"

The wave rose and as it did, so did our intensity. As we moaned and groaned we writhed about in sweaty, sensual abandon. And I'm not ashamed to say that I was nearly making as much noise as her. My dick was tingling and she played this game, grab it, let it go, grab it, let it go, grab it, let go. I stood up, she stood up; I lay down she lay down. Grab it, let it go, grab it, let it go. She bit my chest, my stomach, ahhh. I explored her, I felt inside her, I teased her. She was so wet.

We rolled about and she bit, and she bit me again. I held her arms I pinned her to the floor, breathlessly she moaned, "I'm going to bite you, I'm going to bite you all over. Ahhh, ahhh." Her legs encircled my waist and I could take no more. I drove inside her, I rammed inside her, and lifted her up. I was King Kong, ahhh.

She held me tight, squeezed me tight, bit my neck. I laid her down, jammed her, as she wriggled about like a snake. But I was on her and would not let her go. We humped, we pumped, we humped, we pumped. We came together, but who shouted out the loudest I couldn't swear to. I'll try and keep my dignity and say it was her.

When I had finally recovered, I found that we were in bed. How we got there I don't really know, but you know those sessions where you wonder. I lay on my back, she with her head on my chest, giving me wonderful, sensual kisses, while holding me tight. I was touched. She seemed rather shy in the light of day and I knew immediately that this wasn't a normal occasion for her. I felt quite pleased and chuffed with myself.

It was Saturday morning and the clock said 10:30. I got up to go to the toilet. "You don't have to get up.

We can stay in bed if you want," she said looking at me, smiling, then covering her head in shyness as I stared at her with wide-eyed mock horror at the suggestion. She reappeared from under the blanket and gave me the most gorgeous smile ever.

When I came back to bed she said, "Do you want breakfast in bed?" Then she looked me in the eyes and kissed me. My heart skipped a beat. She gave me a big hug and kiss and took the sheet. I had a smile on my face from ear to ear. Yeah, it didn't get much better than this.

I jumped out of bed to give her a hand but a few hours passed before we settled down to breakfast; we larked and played around like two teenagers in love for the first time. She was special. We spent the rest of the day playing scrabble, monopoly, dominoes, ludo, black jack; I didn't even get upset when she won everything. I let her win, but don't tell her that. We ended up going for a walk in the park. I hate that, but with her, I loved it.

I left Sunday afternoon when she went to pick her son up. She even wanted me to stay and meet him; I promised I would next time. We kissed passionately and said our goodbyes until tomorrow. She offered to drive me to get my car in the West End where it was still parked but I politely declined. I needed time to clear my head. With goodbye, I left.

She really was special. But as I closed her front door behind me, I felt uneasy. I looked up, she was waving at me from the window, it was idyllic. But I couldn't commit to anybody, how could I? Didn't I have unfinished business with the scum who thought he was a bully? As I turned the corner out of sight of Katie I mumbled "Well I'm fucking coming for you son, I'm fucking coming for you."

Standing at the bus stop as the bus approached I thought, *Once again, happiness has eluded me*. Just then my new mobile began to ring. I looked at the number it was Katie; I pressed it off. Why make her unhappy. Then I received a text: I miss you already- Katie

When the bus arrived, I entered and sat down. Again I thought, *What's to become of me*? I missed her too.

AFTER SEVERAL MONTHS of undercover detective work I at last, had found out where the bully lived. Heh! Heh! Heh! Heh! I sat opposite the house in the stolen car that had been re-plated– a dark car that blended into the dark night. At least now I had a plan, proof that I was on my way back, getting myself together. I was going to the gym and eating the right food and had stopped smoking everything.

The piece of shit, I was gonna fuck him up, properly fuck him up. I wasn't going to let him go, no way. He deserved it, he deserved to die and would die, this very night. But somehow the gun didn't seem in tune with me, it didn't feel as if we were on the same wavelength. It was like it didn't want to be there. And *Madness*, where was *Madness*? Normally around this time he would be kicking, shouting and screaming, KILL THE SON OF A BITCH! But *Madness* wasn't around. I didn't panic because *Madness* sometimes crashed the party at the last minute.

The street I was parked on was very quiet, with not much activity.

"Don't do it."

I turned my head around quickly to the back seat, but no one was there of course. It had seemed so clear, could that really have been my sub-conscious kicking in.

"Fuck off!" I said aloud, to whom or what, I don't know, "I'm going to KILL HIM regardless; there's no forgiveness or forgetting. Liberties have been taken, fuck that."

Someone came out from the house and began walking in my direction towards the car. I jumped out, gun behind my back as I approached the person coming towards me. Please, please, please let it be him. But it wasn't. It was a teenager with a black woolly hat, just like mine. As we passed, he looked straight at me, smiled pleasantly, and said in a very mild and friendly voice, "Hello," and kept walking on about his business.

I was slightly taken aback, because there was no mistaking the undeniable resemblance between the polite young person and the bully. Maybe his son even.

Believe it or not, my morals would never allow me to go to a family house to shoot someone in front of their family, no matter how much I believed he deserved it. I went back to the car. I wasn't worried that the young boy had seen me, there was no way he was suspicious or would even link anything together.

In the car my mind began to race. Did I believe in God? Yes, of course I did. Then how could it be possible that I should be sitting outside another human being's house, ready to kill him, to take and end his life? Well this was the law of the jungle, wasn't it? He knew the rules as well as I did. No one's got the right to put their hands on someone else with the intention to harm or maim them. And not only had one person done it to me, but three of them. Bullies, liberty takers, who thought they could go around and terrorise and intimidate people, well I was here to show them differently. When I finished with this guy they would know he had been chastised and that they did things at their peril.

My friends and people I knew would say I was right. Even straight black people in many cases would have no sympathy for him. Because no doubt along the way they would have come up against bullies like that within the community which had humiliated them, their children, or even worse. Well I'm not fucking having it. I got out of the car, walked towards the bully's house gun in hand, and knocked on the fucking door.

THAT NIGHT IN Brixton Hill with Fiss was the beginning of a nightmare. Had I known that Fiss was already strung out on drugs, I would have parted company with him– then again, perhaps not. With the drugs Fiss became unpredictable, not that he wasn't already, or I, for that matter. But he had lost the plot, big time. The drugs had a power and hold over him that led him dancing to a merry tune. Unfortunately he was the only one who heard it. It clouded his judgement and perspective of right and wrong. Any wrong doings or deeds he performed became easily justifiable to him. I tried my best to help him, but like many others, my understanding of hard drugs was very limited at that time.

It was as if we were connected by an electric current. Me with my marital problem, him with whatever demons he had inside plus a drug induced spirit that haunted and tormented him. I didn't abandon him, but it became harder and harder to reason with him. And regardless of the good intentions I once had, I let a lot of my own morals and principles slip. Of course it was never my fault, always someone else's.

So it was, with these false misconceptions, that I found myself in the zone with Fiss.

And then the inevitable happened.

EIGHT

It was 1997. Here I was, back again, in the very place I vowed I would never return– prison.

As my good friend Polly - who was now married with two children, living in the States - said, "Trevor how could you?"

How could I tell her that my whole life was like a war zone, that I was on constant alert for real or imaginary flak. How could I tell her that no matter what I did I felt useless? How could I tell her, I felt as if I didn't belong and always felt uncomfortable? How could I tell her I believe that society is taking the piss out of me everywhere I turn? How could I tell her I was still fighting a battle, a war that I hadn't started?

Worst of all, how could I tell her I am no longer 'normal by society's standards'? How could I tell her? How could I tell her about my innermost turmoil, the many conflicts that grew inside of me like a fire? How could I explain about the *Rage*? The Rage!!!! Rage!!!! Rage!!!!

Here I was again, imprisoned for some nonsense, for like many I believed I could get through life by cheating. By not conforming, I took my rebelliousness and non-conformity as a sign that I was still, as I once was, a good person fighting for change. But as I sat down in that empty cell I knew that the person I once was, had gone. Gone along with certain high standards I once had set myself. Gone with the many principles and morals that I once deemed of the upmost importance to a man, a decent human being. I was not who I started out as, along the way I had become tainted. I had become involved in drugs and violence and other such things that even now are hurtful to recall.

I had changed, and those people around me with goodness could see that change. And they were the ones I hurt the most. I cared nothing for other's feelings, I was obnoxious, unforgiving, ruthless, and most of all, frightening. I was a terror. As I look back I can see why people gradually shied away from me. More often than not, they weren't sure which way I would turn on any given whim. They felt they had to pacify me, fearing I was uncontrollable, and of course that doesn't make for an equal relationship. To put it bluntly, my friends and loved ones were afraid of me.

Society was also afraid of me, but I couldn't have cared less because I deemed myself not part of society. But when my friends and loved ones begin showing signs of fearing me, it was time to look at my life. And

I did as I sat there in that empty cell. I looked at my whole life, my relationship with my friends, loved ones *and* society.

I wanted to be embraced back into society, I wanted to be embraced back into the fold of those I cared about. And very importantly, I didn't want to die, die for some trivial feud because of some macho respect thing. I didn't want to kill just because that was the way on the streets– kill or be killed. I realised this was madness, and this madness was affecting many of us. Like a cancer, it was touching people it had no right to touch, right down to our very young offspring, our *children*.

Since the age of 16, my whole life had been one of ruin, waste, and uncontrollable anger. Memories of being arrested in Porchester Road and then convicted for something I hadn't done, flashed through my mind. That was the first time I'd had any dealings with the police and all at once I realised where much of my anger and hatred had come from.....

Thinking back to the early days and my first conviction, it was all so unbelievable. I had many character references, but because the other two had been in trouble it was assumed I was also a delinquent. Rightly or wrongly, the message I got from the trial at the Old Bailey was that even a drunken white man's word was worth more than mine because there were no other witnesses to what he alleged– attempted robbery.

And when the judge asked, "Where are his parents?"

and none were forthcoming and then they were told I was in a hostel having just been released from a children's home, they decided then of course, I must be guilty. Everything I ever believed in crumbled into small tiny pieces as I stood in that courtroom. As I looked around the room all I saw was white faces. And if I didn't know who I was, I knew who and what I didn't ever want to be. And that was white.

Surely someone would speak up and say no, no, no, there's been a grave mistake. But no-one did. Even the lawyer representing me didn't put up a good show and avoided eye contact whenever possible. It was traumatic enough walking into court, never mind standing in the dock. But when the judge said, "Guilty!" I wanted the ground to open up and swallow me. I burned all over with shame. I felt hot, dizzy and sick. This was the worst thing that had ever happened to me ever.

Even at the children's homes, when others stole sweets I would never. I would never ever dream of it. I had never stolen anything in my whole life. It was a sin. It was that simple to me. I even told them in the court that I was a Roman Catholic but no-one batted an eye lid. I then realised that no-one really cared who or what I was, I was guilty. It was blatantly obvious, the system I had just been through had no respect for me at all. This, too, filled me with shame, great shame. When I left that courthouse, I left a different person.

The police had come to my cell wearing black gloves. Then they began slapping me, punching me, saying I should write a statement against myself and the others. They started calling me names such as: coon, nigger, jungle bunny. I had tears in my eyes. Not from the physical stuff, that was easy. I had been in children's homes where priest and staff at any given time took it upon themselves to give you a backhander. The tears were because I felt like I was less than a human being.

They made me feel that I should feel that I didn't belong here in this country. Yet I was born here, and knew nothing else. As far as I was concerned this *was* my country. But they were to make me aware for the first time what Alf Garnet really meant. Before, it was just some TV comedy character taking the mickey out of someone. But the police made me realise, that it was an evil thing, a thing of hate. It was a scary thing to think that these were the people that I was raised as a child to respect.

It would not have been so bad had it been one or two who had treated me that way. But it was most of them, and they did it openly; they didn't give a hoot. And those that hadn't join in smiled and laughed along with the others.

Not one person said a word in dissent of what was being said and done to me, a 16-year-old boy.

As I've always said, I hate bullies and people who have the power and abuse it. I have seen enough of that throughout my life in childcare. As I watched those police officers they were the scum of the earth to me. They were the lowest life form on the face of the planet. They were to me, all McCann's brothers, all family, all related. All scum.

NINE

I knocked again but louder this time; still no one answered the door. I had been standing outside knocking on the bully's door for about a minute, so I decided to go back to the car. I had worked myself up so much that I had given myself a headache.

Once back in the car, I decided to drive off and head home. My heart was thumping and I was covered in sweat.

Just as I was about to take a right turn, a car came out of nowhere and skidded, then stalled, in front of me. My first reaction was to grab my gun as I thought things might get heated. But it turned out to be a really old bloke, about seventy. He was bald, with thick rimmed glasses and was driving a Mazda. The shock of it all made me wind down the window and say, "What the fuck you doing old man?" But then I felt sorry for him and realised what I had in my possession.

"Sorry old man; just the heat of the moment."

He looked at me and said, "Go on, fuck off"

As I started laughing, he opened his door to get out but almost fell out. The guy was completely drunk. I put the pedal to the floor and was out of there. In my rearview mirror I could see the old boy shaking his fist in anger at my departure. All of this brought a smile to my face and gradually all the tension subsided.

When I got home I put my tracksuit and trainers on, placed my headphones in position and put on a woolly hat. I selected a tape and was out the front door.

Just as I began my run, Paul Weller shouted, "...*Sup up your beer and collect your face, there's a row going on down near Slough....*" As I got into the running I smiled. I loved The Jam, *Eton Rifles*, *Going underground*, I just loved their vibrant music. But most of all I loved the lyrics. I was away 'inside' when they first came out. But had I been around I would definitely have gone to one of their concerts even if it meant wearing dark glasses. If they had National Front fans I couldn't care less.

As I pounded on, on, on, I thought *what was I, who was I*? I was trying to change my life around, get myself together. Still, I had the intention of killing a man. Hadn't I promised myself that I would live my life away from all that crap? Hadn't I promised myself during the last prison stretch that I would change my life around?

I ran and I ran and I ran. But I couldn't get away

from Paul Weller "...*I'm down in the tube station at midnight...*" And my mind drifted off into the past to 1997 and a four year sentence in the Scrubs.

Wormwood Scrubs had changed somewhat since I had last been there in the mid seventies. Gone was that austere, foreboding drabness, replaced by gentle, freshly-painted colours. And the place seemed clean and tidy. Not at all as I remembered it so many years before. But despite its new appearance, the place still had an air of trepidation, an undercurrent of menace that followed you with every step. There was something wrong within this prison; it was like someone was laughing at you but you couldn't see them. The laughter echoed off the walls along the passages and hung like a cloud or a spectre in the air. There was something amiss here.

The guards - the screws - seemed young to me and they were. In the seventies, prison officers strutted about in immaculate uniforms; everything highly polished, it was an aggressive military style of intimidation. Rules were rules; you didn't need to ask any questions, everything was black or white, there were no grey areas. Either you were entitled or you weren't. It went by the letter of law: the rules. You knew where you stood. You knew what you were allowed to do and where you were allowed to be at any given time; there wasn't much call for interaction between them and us. They stayed away from us and we stayed away from them and that's the way it was.

But these screws, though a younger breed, walked around as if they were proper bods. They swaggered about as if they themselves were the villains. "What you looking at, you want some?" They tried to give off a streetwise persona. In other words, they were a 'firm.' A firm that didn't have to play by anyone else's rules as long as they got the job done, got it sorted.

"Who cares, fuck 'em," was the order of the day. They had the street jargon down to a 'T', and it was not a hard job visualising them as a firm of gangsters.

I had been allocated to a double cell with a Scottish guy. Even though we didn't seem to have much in common we tried to make the best of it, as you do when you come to prison. I met a few old faces for whom jail had become an occupational hazard and in many cases an inevitability. *Welcome home son.*

The number of black people inside this prison was unbelievable. It was predominantly black and my immediate thoughts were that of television programmes I had seen from the States were it seemed they put *all* black people in prison. It was coming to pass that the jails here too, would be filled with black men.

One of the most astounding things was that there were now female prison officers. This was just unbelievable. Of course, there weren't that many and for the most part they somehow seemed gentler, more easy going than their male counterparts. But lo and behold should one take a disliking to you; then you knew you were in trouble. The male screws had a chivalrous white knight in shining armour' attitude, aligned with this male thing that a woman couldn't do anything without their help. So, many inmates avoided women screws but of course it didn't stop one from looking, and thinking *if only....* Some women officers played on this and could, at will, instigate trouble just to show her male colleagues that she too, was part of the firm. Largely it was many cocks trying to impress a few hens.

I met up with a few guys with whom we had served time back in the seventies. For us, it was a culture shock. I can't believe I'm saying this but it's like we had become the old lags. The ones who had seen it, done it, got the t-shirts, been this route before. We were afforded a modicum of respect, but unlike the old days these young guys respected few.

As I walked around the exercise yard with an old friend by the name of Pat, it suddenly dawned on us what the uneasy feeling was. The place was like a hospital. It appeared that the majority of people in the prison were into drugs in one form or another. As we walked around the exercise yard there were people doing all kinds of drug deals. Some huddled in clusters, some gaunt and zombified, the whole prison culture seemed to be one of drugs.

In the prison I knew before, if someone had a bit of puff it was usually for personal use and you might give a friend a draw. But here, people in this very jail sold cannabis, marijuana, cocaine, heroin, and crack. And made money from it. Just like they would outside on the street.

In simple terms, the jail was being run by drug dealers, people who sold drugs for a profit and they had many customers. People who may never have had dealings with drugs could now acquire a habit or what it was termed a "prison habit." They'd say, "I'm only doing it while I'm in here." Yeah right! And those who *had* indulged while on the outside now found they could also now indulge on the inside providing they had the cash or something to barter.

I BRING MYSELF BACK to the present. I reached home and the sweat was pouring off me. I switched off Paul Weller and lay spread-eagle on my front step. I felt good, I had the power, I felt like a new man, I felt wonderful.

The phone rang inside and against my better judgement, I got up to answer it.

"Hello?" I said into my mobile.

"Hello Trevor."

I froze, unable to move. My heart started to beat really fast.

"I've missed you."

I still didn't answer, but she talked on.

"I don't know what the problem is but we can sort it out. I know how you feel about me Trevor, and I'm sure it's not another woman. Are you going to talk to me at all, or do I have to bite you?"

I began to laugh and she began to laugh. I was happy inside, even though I knew I had no right to be. But I missed her.

"How are you? Your voice sounds sexy."

She laughed and said in a husky patois, "You t'ink so?"

And I duly replied, "Yeah man, you sound rude."

There was warmth in our laughter, there was a

spark of electricity in the air.

But most of all there was sex, hot sex in the air and we both knew it.

"Are you coming round?" she said.

"Yeah."

"How long?"

"I'll be there in an hour-and-a-half."

"See you then."

The phone went dead, and I just stood there and thought.

It had been several weeks since our first and only meeting. I had never gone back, or rung her. She had rung me twice, I never answered, and after that she had not rung again. Though I thought of her often, I could not bring myself to call her. But standing with the phone in my hand and a warm glow inside me, I realised how much I had missed her.

Now at least, I was able to feel comfortable going out with a woman. I was dressed well, I had a bit of money, and I had a car. I was quite together. But there was still the problem of the bully.

A quick bath, skin cream, some Joop aftershave, and I was heading for the front door.

SHE OPENED THE door dressed in a long dashiki and a smile so warm and inviting it made the whole house cosy. As I came through the front door a soul classic was playing (Too late to turn back now.).

My mamma told me son please beware... floated from the speakers and without a word we both came together and began dancing. Oh, how I wish I could fully describe how wonderful it felt. But I was scared of the emotions that were flooding through me. I don't know who kissed who, but I remember tasting her salty tears.

The music was playing, ...*Dreams are for those who dream, I wanna make it with you*...all of a sudden the sensual turned sexual. We began to wind up and wind down, her leg pressed more and more into my groin and I pressed my leg between hers and began a rub-a-dub style of my own. But she knew it and came back with a style that began to bend me up. I held my corner, and before I knew it we were having sex on the couch. When I began mouthing, "Your son..." she replied curt and to the point breathlessly. "–Camping." And she pushed herself up ready for the t'ing. Bam, bam, ram, ram.

The next thing I knew we had moved to the bedroom and were making slow, lingering love. She whispered, "I love you." What possessed me I don't know but I replied, "I love you too baby." We fell asleep in each others arms and again I dreamt of where I was coming from.

Back To 1997 in Scrubs. I dreamt of a past life that somehow still seemed to effect my present life indirectly. If I could understand my past, I might just be able to help myself for the future.

TROUBLE, AS IT HAD a habit of doing, soon found yours truly. It was as if we were old friends who hadn't seen each other for a while. But these days it was different. I was a reluctant participant and could usually look ahead, thus avoiding a reunion.

But on the day in question I was blissfully unaware that for some time I had been under observation by the head honcho of the screws who thought of themselves as the "firm."

Looking back now, it seems obvious that at some stage, some point, there was bound to be some form of confrontation. I had been involved in criminal activity most of my life and had spent time here. I knew deep down that I have never been able to take orders well and have always had problems with authoritarian people.

I'M SORRY TO say that I, along with several of my friends, had bad reputations for fighting, for violence and for standing for no shit. And when I had finished serving my previous seven year sentence, I wrote a book that was published about what it was like being a black man incarcerated for seven years, so you can imagine that among the inmates I was somewhat notorious.

It was known I wasn't a grass; I could keep my mouth shut and above all I was loyal. And though a black guy, I could easily make the transition from the black group to the white group; I always mingled well. Not much of a C.V. you may think, but in the world of villainy and crime these were admirable qualities that were forever stamped on your forehead for everyone to see.

Fortunate for me, one or two guys I knew worked behind the hot-plate and my own plate was always generously piled high while the screw who usually stood behind the hot-plate watched in silence. There wasn't much he could say as I wasn't getting extra portions -when he was watching- its just that I was getting the maximum portion. The screw was a horrible man whom I nicknamed Goatee. He was abusive to almost everyone, he was a bully.

I watched Goatee sizing me up, and on one or two occasions he tried to engage me in conversation. I say conversation but it was usually a sly dig at another prisoner. For example he'd say, "Get a move on or I'll get Hercules on to you."

I never once spoke to him, just carried on walking. He was testing me but I just wasn't having it; he wanted to see what I was made of. He wanted some of what I had, street cred; to be one of the boys, to hang out with the boys.

All the guys who worked on the hot-plate were 'his boys' and his greatest joy would be to get guys like me to work for him on the hot-plate. But as I said, I wasn't having none of it, I just wanted to get on with my sentence and get out. I was no longer a 21-year-old youth who would bite at the slightest provocation. I was in my forties and much dismayed at my present plight and dare I say slightly humiliated to find myself back here again amongst guys some of whom I was old enough to have fathered.

THE ALARM BELL constantly rang as screws in blue uniforms tore about the place to the source of trouble.

At these times you were locked up, but the screams of the helpless prisoner would ring out loud and clear. Even if they couldn't lock us up while they dragged and kicked a prisoner to the block, not one prisoner would open their mouth.

It seemed incredible that these screws could do what they liked without repercussions. They couldn't and wouldn't have acted so blatantly in the old days, the cons would never have stood for it. But like I said before, prison had changed. It was now like a hospital and most of the people in here were on drugs. Prisons now even had drug-free wings for those who could not be around drugs at all. And everyone in the prison had random drugs tests. Drugs had become so rife in prison that it was now the main topic of conversation.

As I stood in line to see the doctor, a friend of mine Dave - who worked in the clothing store about 10 yards from where I stood - invited me to quickly come over and get a pair of new trousers and a shirt. Just as I reached the store, Goatee, who had been watching unbeknownst to me, came over and started shouting at me.

"You're not supposed to be there! Get in line! You don't go anywhere unless I tell you, got it."

I walked back to the line without a word. Many people had seen him shouting at me and I was really embarrassed. When it was my turn to see the doctor and Goatee called my name, I walked up to him and said that I had changed my mind and I didn't want to see the doctor after all. We stood staring at each other, I had been here before, many times.

"Get back to your cell then."

"That's where I wanna go".

"Go on then".

"Yeah, all right, I'm going."

But I didn't go. I stood there staring at him, as he did me, for what seemed an eternity. Parts of my life flashed in front of me; people I hadn't seen since childhood now seemed the most important people in the world to me. And the one prevailing thought I had was wondering what death would be like. How the spell was broken between us I don't know, but praise the Lord. All I can recall was heading for the stairs and him saying, "You're not big enough Hercules."

And still I persisted. "Yeah, yeah, sure."

When I reached my cell I lay down on my bed. I felt a bit shaky, but I felt good. Because I knew they wouldn't be coming for me this time, but deep down I knew it was only a matter of time before they would.

TEN

We both came awake about the same time; both on our sides, facing each other, looking into each other's eyes and smiling.

"Scared," she said.

"Scared of what?"

"You know, scared of getting involved, scared of getting hurt, I don't know. I just know there's something holding you back, but for the life of me I don't know what."

"Why are you women so forward?"

She kissed my nose. "You'll keep," she replied then snuggled up to me.

From somewhere, soft reggae music began to play, it was 7.30 in the morning. And may I say all was well in the camp. While I held her in my arms, I began to contemplate what it would be like, to wake up to this every morning. But from an early age, my life has been one disappointment after another. I truly believed now that I didn't have that much control over my emotions of love. And whether or not I wanted to love her or give myself to her, it wasn't that easy.

My mobile rang, and I answered it.

"Yes, alright, of course I was up. Did you think I would still be in bed? I'll see you in an hour-and-a-half."

I began to stretch.

"I've got to go out baby, just some business."

"Who was that, your girlfriend?" she said smiling, then poking out her tongue.

She knew it wasn't a girl because she had listened to every word being said, weighed them up, dissected them, turned them around and deciphered them; all the while registering my body language. She, like most women, did all this quite nonchalantly, as if she wasn't listening, as if she didn't care. But brother, she knew exactly what was going on.

"Business, what type of business honey, baby?"

I jumped out of bed laughing.

"Oh Yeah, oh Yeah, here we go."

But still smiling, all she said was, "You'll keep."

We were on the dance floor jumping up to McFadden and Whitehead's, *Ain't no stopping us now* when Katie first asked me what I did for a living. We had just met. At the time I was drunk, and with the money Frank had given me, and my new Saab, I felt I was back to my old self; so I replied: criminal activity. She had already told me that she was a solicitor, so I asked for her card and number... just in case.

Whether she fully believed me or not I don't know, I can't say, but I do feel she knew there was some truth to what I had told her. Anyway, she said, "Come on," and we went back to her table where her friends sat nudging and smiling at each other and pretending nothing was going on. All the while they were looking me over, seeing if I had potential for their friend. But you know how it goes boys, I got in first.

"What would you lovely ladies like to drink? We danced the night away.

KATIE COOKED ME plantain and eggs with toast and coffee and sat opposite, watching me as I ate. She made me feel heavenly and she knew it.

"Are you all right baby?"

Now she was fluttering her eye lids, and there were butterflies in my stomach. The radio was playing, *Hey there, lonely girl, lonely girl...* and I wished it would stop... *hey there lonely girl let me mend you broken heart like new.*

We were in the middle of the kitchen kissing passionately now, and as I held her, I never ever wanted to let her go. We arranged to meet up later in the day around two but I would ring just to confirm. As I closed the door behind me, she opened the upstairs window and shouted, "I'm going to have you!"

My thoughts flashed back to the old white man in the car. I shouted up, "No black bastard!" She gave me a quizzical look, as if I were mad, then said, "I miss you already." I blew her a kiss and got into my ride. And I felt good.

I met Frank outside Whitechapel Station at nine thirty, we got into his car. Immediately he said,"I've got a bit of a problem, we'll go to a café and I'll tell you all about it." When Frank said he had a problem, what he meant was, there was trouble, real trouble. I settled down in the car, and thought to myself, *I wonder where it will all end?*

We pulled up outside the café and got out. The sun was poking through the clouds; it might not be such a bad day after all.

I AM AN ANGRY MAN, I'm a very angry man, I've been angry for most of my life. Once upon a time I truly believed that I had a direction for my anger and could really justify it. But as time has gone by, I have come to realise that I am a dangerous individual waiting to explode.

I have no allegiance to any country for I have no country. I have no allegiance to any leader because I have no leader. I, like may others, am living in limbo where everything is not black and white, but WHITE.

It's like I once explained to my white friend Ian. Imagine you found yourself in Africa and everywhere you turned you saw black faces. They spoke African languages, the government and all the institutions were run by black people, the programmes they showed on television were black, the whole country was black orientated. Then across the water you saw people like you suffering and you knew the people where you lived, in Africa, had the technology and know-how to stop most of that suffering; how would you feel? Ian's reply was that it was his worst nightmare.

Still, I had had my chances. Looking back at my missed opportunities, I felt ashamed. I was an apprentice electrician at the age of 16 and doing day release at college to study it. That I was made redundant should never have been a problem, I could have found another apprenticeship if I had really wanted to, I could have gone on to be a technician or something else. But no, I thought there was something out on the streets for me, and there was– a wasted life. I was at journalist college and guess what? I left because outside I thought others were having the time of their lives doing villainy. Many of those who finished the course went on to good jobs in the BBC and other places. And they were not all coconuts, believe me, some of them are proud black people, family orientated. And me? Well, just let me tell you a life of crime isn't worth it, no matter what gripe you think you may have against a society that you believe alienates you.

Trust me, there is nothing like self-respect, love of self, to help make you feel good and clean inside. And it is an option, but it means change. You may have to go through a lot before you realise that change, but it *is* possible. I can change, I will. But there are a few obstacles to overcome first.

ELEVEN

The screw stood at the bottom of the stairs barring my way. I stood opposite him not more than six inches away and we stared at each other. All that I could think of, over and over again was, I don't need this.

The screw who stood in front of me was about 5', I am 5' 11". He was Goatee's side-kick, part of a double act like Little and Large, Eric and Ernie, Miss Piggy and Kermit. He had jet black hair slicked back and an effeminate manner. If it wasn't such a serious situation, one could almost double up with laughter and just say, "Piss off."

It was early in the morning, breakfast time. In one hand I held a plastic plate upon which was my breakfast; in the other, a cup of boiling hot water from the urn with which to make my tea.

When situations such as this arise it astounded me how my brain could produce images I hadn't consciously conjured up. I was treated to a kaleidoscope of beautiful scenes of freedom: open spaces in the sun, fields covered in an assortment of wonderfully blooming flowers. Next, like a bird, I was flying through the air with the sun shining on me in a cloudless blue sky. So surreal.

"Move out of the way, please."

I didn't say that I'm sure, but my lips had moved.

"Move out of the way, please."

Again, my body was reacting with a mind of its own.

My right hand rose slowly until the cup of boiling water rested next to my chest in a gesture that could be construed as threatening. Perhaps I should have told the screw that my body had a life of its own and that this, what I can only describe as a futile gesture, had nothing to do with me at all. But in an instant he had jumped aside, and my feet took me up the stairs.

My cell was on the three's landing, but before I had reached it my cellmate was behind me.

"They're gonna be coming, their definitely coming. They're gonna come up, they'll be here soon."

The guy was bordering on the hysterical and who could blame him; certainly not me. He knew as well as I that they would be coming, and coming mob handed. Anything in the way would be crushed; it was their way of instilling the fear of God into everyone. Their rule was the rule of violence.

The breaking of any prison rule, or any kind of trouble would be dealt with by the Governor. Ordinarily you would be placed on report and in the morning brought before the Governor. This was called judication but *this* mob were judge and jury. And after they finished with you then the Governor could have you. That's just as long as you weren't too badly injured. They would definitely be coming this time.

Three minutes later, with most of the other prisoners locked away, they came. I heard them as they stampeded up the grated metal staircases like a herd of buffalo. I hadn't touched my breakfast, and I had remained standing from the minute I had entered my cell. Why, I don't know. Perhaps some primeval instinct for survival that said one should be standing during conflict. You know, something akin to not getting caught-short with your trousers down.

The door flew open and standing at the head of the queue was the sissy. He advanced just inside the doorway as the others bunched up behind him straining at their leashes. As he stood in the doorway he was visibly shaking as he began to rant, "You tried to throw hot water over me," he said several times. Each time he said it, I denied it.

This went on for a while, just like a tennis match, backwards and forwards. He was the only one of them who spoke. But as this seemed to be going nowhere the screws behind him began trying to jostle him forward towards me, but he was having none of it. It was apparent what was going on. It was his collar and he was to be the first to steam in. But Sissy was in limbo. Should I go or should I stay, should I twist or should I bust? Throughout it all he stuck to his theme.

"You tried to throw hot water on me, you tried to throw hot water on me." It was becoming more of a whine now, more of a plea for me to agree to it. But you know me, I'm a stubborn bastard, and if God himself had come down at that very moment I think I would still have denied it. By now he was almost in tears, and as he wilted I grew stronger, taller, more powerful by the second.

When the thunder of their footsteps began the ascend to my cell I was scared. Not scared of them. I had been in similar positions outside, and in prison before my last sentence. Myself and friends had fought guys with knives and had run-ins with people with guns. No, it wasn't the fight that I feared, it was the possibility that I might squeal or bawl out when they started beating me up and took me away. I considered this a weakness.

When they hauled people away, they took great pride in bending the person up so that the inmates could hear their screams and wails of pain. This was a psychological ploy on their part; there's not a more chilling thing than to hear a grown man scream out in pain. And they took much pleasure and delight in this, it was always a source of amusement and added to their macho self-image. But the longer I stood there, the more powerful I became. In truth, it would have taken a million men to make me scream out this day. I had the power. And the power that emanated from me bounced everywhere within that cell. My fear had faded.

With impatient frustration at the lack of activity, one of the screws from the middle of the pack bustled his way past Sissy into the middle of the cell, and now stood facing me. It was Goatee.

"You think your someone special but no one's special in this nick!"

He was shouting, but his voice lacked that hyped up adrenaline intensity that usually accompanied a violent act. It seemed his whole persona was born more out of frustration at his colleagues inept display rather than a violent disposition towards me. The moment was lost and the bravado they had displayed in the beginning had drained away with each passing moment of inactivity. The sissy's face now held the look of defeat; he obviously wasn't up to the job.

"Pack your kit, you're on basics," said Goatee, as they watched me pack my stuff together.

I was marched down onto the two's landing and into the office—each landing had its own. The landing officer, who sat behind the desk, was what you would call without hesitation, a flash bastard. He thought he was God's gift and he probably was where eh came from—Mars.

Screwing his face up into his best effort of a bad man, he related that while on basics he would be watching me. But I could see he was impressed that I had managed to come down in one piece. Through it all, I said not one word. I was escorted to basics which was about eight cells at the end of the two's landing, slightly apart from the two's main cells.

All this prison jargon was all new to me. Fifteen years on, the only punishment *I* knew was the block. What was this basics all about I wondered as they unlocked the door to a cell. But wait a minute, there was someone's card outside, surely they weren't going to put me in a cell with someone else. But sure enough, when they opened the door there was already an inmate in there. What the fuck was going on?

After they deposited me in the cell and closed the door, I stood with my back against the wall suspiciously eyeing my new cellmate.

"Trevor, Trevor, it's me."

I looked closely and saw that it was a black guy from Ladbroke Grove whom I knew reasonably well, but not that well.

"What's going on? What's all this?"

He could see I was wary and he did his best to allay my apprehension about what I thought might be happening.

"Nothing's happening Trevor, you're on basics, this is it."

"What do you mean this is it?" said I, loosening up a bit.

"That's all there is to it Trevor. They just keep you here for a week or two until they're ready to let you back on normal location."

"Are you kidding me or what?"

Looking around the cell I noticed he still had his radio and other such luxuries. He began to explain that basics just meant that you were removed from normal location as a punishment and after a while one or two weeks usually they let you back into normal circulation. Well you could have knocked me down with a feather, this was just unbelievable.

"This is not punishment. What's happened to the

block?" (The block, annexed from the main prison, was dark and dingy. You stayed on your own and were allowed no privileges, certainly not your radio, and they made your time as unpleasant as possible.)

"They only use it as a last resort T. You don't want to go there."

I relaxed and settled in. We talked for a few hours. It seemed the whole of Ladbroke Grove was in here; some drug bust clear up. After a while I layed down on my bed (still couldn't believe I still *had* my bed) and as is my want, I drifted off into a different world. Still got my bed and didn't even get bashed, things were looking up. But with me, there's always trouble around the corner it seems, and it wasn't finished with me, not just yet. As I drifted off to sleep, that nagging feeling of regret returned. I didn't have to be here; what a waste.

OKAY, BACK TO THE PRESENT. The café was quite clean, and despite there being several customers, we found an empty table. Frank had ordered a large breakfast, and as I had already eaten, I just took tea. Frank and myself had met several times since the first time I went to his place. And as I watched him tuck into his breakfast, every so often he would scan the room.

"Are we looking for someone in here Frank?"

"Nah, not really, but I was hoping this fellow might come in. I need someone to drive an articulated lorry in a hurry. The problem is Trev, someone's taken the piss. I paid this guy thirty grand for a parcel and still haven't got it."

"You mean you paid thirty grand up front?"

"Yeah, I know, don't say anymore please!"

"You do know where to find him, don't you?"

"Yeah, well that's the thing, I do and I don't. But I know where his partner is. And someone's given me information that he will be bringing in a parcel this afternoon at one o'clock on the lorry, but I'm going to take that load."

"How reliable is the information?"

"Very. Anyway, I need someone to drive the lorry at short notice. Like *now*."

"Why not get hold of him and let him tell you where his partner is?"

"I've spoken to him twice and he says he doesn't know, but I've been told he does know and I've had enough of them pulling my plonker. I need that money *now* because a lot of my money is tied up in something else. The gear in there, I was able to get it sold on, straight away and I need that money.

"I got someone, let's go to the phone box," I said.

We sat waiting in the car, the three of us: me, Frank and the person who was going to drive the lorry, lets just call him Billy. We were just off the motorway, parked up with a good view of a very large warehouse.

"That's the one," Frank said and immediately followed the lorry onto the motorway. We knew exactly where he'd stop, and he did, at a certain motorway restaurant. You can imagine his shock when he returned to his lorry to be met by me and

Billy. Frank couldn't show his face; it was his bit of work and he didn't want any comebacks.

With the original driver blindfolded and tied up, we drove to our designated point to unload. After dumping the lorry, we dropped the guy off somewhere to make his own way back and then headed to a pub in Kingsbury - owned by a friend of Frank's - where we began quietly celebrating and waiting for a man to come and weigh Frank in with the readies. Billy and I didn't really want to meet him, but when Frank called his name, he was someone I knew well. He was a very nice guy; I had been 'away' with him.

"What about the thirty grand?" I asked Frank.

"As far as I'm concerned he still owes me my money. He doesn't know this is down to me; he'll never know. I've found out he's rumped so many people, no wonder he's hiding. People are looking for him everywhere. It's a pity I didn't know this before. Rumour has it that he's got a bad gambling habit. His Missus left him and apparently knew where most of his money was and stole it. Then she went on the missing list."

"Besides," Frank said laughing, "that bit of work has got nothing to do with me, two black guys nicked his lorry, what's that got to do with me?"

We all laughed and raised our glasses and Billy countered, "Are we really black, Trevor?" and we fell about laughing.

We got paid, not as much as we first thought, but a nice amount. The person who gave us the keys and information had to get paid as well. After some drunk male bonding between the three of us, we said our goodbyes, hugging each other.

"I love you son."

"Keep it real."

"Keep it sweet."

We left the back room of the pub in Kingsbury and went outside.

Earlier, I had explained to Katie that I would not be able to make it for the afternoon. But as soon as we finished the bit of work, I rang her from the pub. My excuse for ringing her was that I was drunk.... and I was. She suggested gleefully she would meet me at Kingsbury Station. I didn't object. Especially when she said she feared I might - being drunk - be tempted to drive. It coincided quite nicely that we finished our business at nine thirty. I had arranged for her to pick me up at the station at ten. Anyway, she got there at quarter to ten just as I arrived, all smiles. I was carrying my plastic bag with my loot.

She could see I was happy and in a very lovely mood and she took liberties. Nice, nice liberties. For example, when we reached her place it wasn't her place at all, but mine. She had quizzed me, and in my drunken state got the information out of me. I had told her before I don't take women to my place, but she just laughed. She took the keys, opened the front door, went straight to the clothes cupboard and started rummaging through. On finding no evidence of any females' presence, she began hugging me, saying she loved me. I waited for her to use the bathroom, then while she was out of sight, I hid my money. Not that I didn't trust her, but it was best she didn't know.

Waiting for her to come out of the bathroom I fell asleep, but awoke to find she had packed all my dirty clothes, curtains, sheets and bedclothes in bin liners to take home and wash in the machine. She threw away lots of stuff, stuff that quite frankly had seen better days. This woman definitely had my interests at heart, and my heart went out to her. She brought me something to eat, it tasted like chicken. My head was spinning; I conked out.

TWELVE

Most of the people in this jail weren't real villains or gangsters. They were opportunists who did anything they could do on the outside to acquire money to buy drugs. And some of the crimes that they had committed were of such an unsavoury nature that the screws thought many of the prisoners were real scum.

The screws were frantic to stop the flow of drugs through "their prison." Visiting time rarely passed without incident. There was always some form of struggle, as the screws descended upon a prisoner before he managed to plug his drugs. This more often than not ended with the prisoner being dragged away for a strip search. And many a time the visitor would be taken away as well, only to be charged with bringing drugs into the prison.

You see many prisoners now seemed unable to do

their bird - their time - unless they had some form of escapism which often came in the form of hard drugs. Imagine people coming off the street with crack-cocaine and heroin habits; they would be tearing the walls down. Any drug dealer inside could make himself a tidy sum. It was paradise, a ready-made market. And for those who had difficulty 'doing their bird,' what better way of passing the time than in a drug-induced stupor.

But many people who weren't on drugs when they came in, soon were by the time they left. Such was the loneliness, boredom, peer pressure and frightening, claustrophobic atmosphere, that many so-called 'straight' inmates started looking for a release, an escape from the pressure. They usually started off doing a little bit so they could sleep or calm their nerves. They could be heard saying, "I'm only doing it while I'm in here." But by the time they left, more often than not, they had acquired a habit.

In the seventies and early eighties one could sometimes find marijuana in prisons. Not that the screws turned a blind eye, but for the most part they weren't so bothered. Marijuana made you mellow and chilled out and wasn't accompanied by bullying, violence, and stealing. With the advent of hard drugs came the bullying, violence, theft and a host of unscrupulous characters. For a small bag of heroin you could pay a junkie to do almost anything you wanted.

Part of the problem was that the prison authorities had introduced the piss test. Randomly or upon suspicion, you would be taken to an enclosure and asked to produce a urine sample. This was sent away for analysis and within three days the results came back. If the results were positive, you automatically served an additional 14 to 28 days. The thing was, marijuana stayed in the blood for up to 28 days, while hard drugs - heroin and cocaine - only three days. And to refuse a piss test was an automatic admission of guilt.

The way in which some inmates tried to defeat the piss test, at times bordered on the ingenious. Some carried someone else's untainted urine in small vials attached to their penis with string, others carried concoctions between the cheeks of their bum and sprinkled it into the sample. When they came to take you for a piss test you were always searched, so you carried nothing in your pockets. It was always a humiliating affair, as the screws tended to try and see that you were actually urinating into the tube without any funny business. Failing to urinate, even if you couldn't, resulted in loss of remission.

EVENTUALLY I MET Katie's son Marvin, a 12-year-old boy with a passion for Arsenal. Being a Spurs supporter myself, we spent many hours debating and teasing each other about our respective football teams. Katie happily looked on at our what my friend Polly would say were our 'Kodak moments.' The three of us did many things and went many places including coach tours, seaside trips, and of course football matches.

Katie had explained to Marvin, who had a good relationship with his father, "Trevor's not taking the place of your dad, Nigel will always be your dad. But you know I care for Trevor, and we've been seeing a lot of each other."

I had met Nigel and got on well with him.

"I know Mum, Trevor's all right. Me and dad have already had a talk, it's okay Mum. I just want you to be happy, so does Dad."

No sooner had he said that, he turned to me and said, "Come on Trev, there's a match on Sky." He turned on his heel and headed for the T.V. room.

Katie looked at me with a huge grin, shrugged her shoulders and said, "He most definitely approves of you."

I followed Marvin into the front room, and got comfortable as the match began. But try as I might I couldn't concentrate on the game before me. I was on a roller coaster that wouldn't stop, just kept on gathering momentum. I was plagued by the knowledge that I had unfinished business that *had* to be taken care of, yet the relationship was moving so quickly. I was slightly confused.

It occurred to me that my only choice might be to jump off the speeding roller coaster, and take my chances before people got hurt, especially Marvin. True he had his father, but hurting his mother would be the same as hurting him. And of course I couldn't and wouldn't do that. We discussed the relationship and it was proposed that we should take things slow. Both of us were conscious that a young boy's feelings would also be involved. But despite the fact we had not been going out that long, we could not hide how we felt. "Trevor, I am committed to making this relationship work," she'd said. Her eyes were on me to move the relationship on to the next level.

Katie had helped me rise above my fear of establishing a loving relationship and I must confess, she helped me to forget. But as I sat in front of the television watching without seeing, I knew I had reached a crucial point in my life, the fork in the road.

Was I really going to sacrifice this to take the bully's life, was I really?

I became steely eyed, taut and rigid, and my mind went into overdrive. The law of the jungle rose up; it had been my philosophy for many years. An eye for an eye. Any liberty had to be avenged; it was a challenge to my manhood. And in this society, this white society, all I *had* was my manhood, whatever that really meant.

Marvin said something to me I didn't hear so I just nodded my head. I went out into the hallway, put my coat on and went through the front door. Katie, who had been cooking, opened the window and shouted something about coming back for dinner. I didn't turn around but raised my hand to acknowledge her. Then drove off.

I thought about Katie and Marvin as I drove around aimlessly, going nowhere in particular.

How could I trust any woman again after what had happened to me—the pain, agony, and torment that had driven me off the rails and turned me into a raging bull. Was I really able to give myself to a woman again? I wasn't sure. All I knew was that I couldn't go through that again.

After about a two hour drive, I found myself outside my flat. Once inside, I put my gloves on and opened my secret compartment. I took out the gun. I say *the* gun, because for the first time I realised it was no longer an extension of me; I didn't want it.

I put the gun back in the compartment, lay down on the bed and drifted off.

Three years probation and a fine– for nothing, for absolutely nothing. And nothing could compare to the stigma and shame of being convicted for attempted robbery at 16-years-old. Where does one go from there? With that label attached to me, I soon realised the answer: back again.

About two weeks after the trial, the firm I was working for went bust and I was made redundant. I left the hostel I was in at the time. Not only had it become unbearable, but things were now different somehow, as of course, I was.

I moved from place to place, or was moved from place to place, by the social care authorities. I soon realised there were many others like me, who had been wronged, who had been mentally and physically abused. Most of us came from children's homes and had scars and issues which we couldn't even begin to comprehend, let alone deal with. Thrown into a world we didn't fully understand, we were left at the mercy of those in society who had respect, those who could and did make our lives a misery, such as the police.

Anyone, at anytime, could call the police on us as black youngsters. Regardless of what it was, we were always in the wrong and more often than not carted off. So every respected citizen knew that if they didn't like us, didn't want us walking along their street, or coming into their shop all they had to do was pick up the phone and call the police. There was no two sides to the story, only theirs.

By this time most of us had been criminalised with some bullshit charge. Usually some concocted story about assaulting the police. Imagine, one young black person standing in the dock while eight burly policemen all claimed to have been assaulted; it was laughable, especially when the youngster was battered and bruised. They really took the piss. I must say that there were *some* white people who stood up against this bullshit, but they were in the minority.

I met up with Dave and the others in a Salvation hostel in Seymour Place, Marylebone. We shared the same outrage at the injustices heaped upon us and endeavoured to find out why people - white people - should wish to treat us this way. Because we couldn't understand it. What was the reason?

In our search for the truth, we read about slavery and colonisation. We were truly horrified. Now we understood why so many white people thought they were better than we were. We now knew why people called us wogs, coons, black bastards. You see, being in children's homes locked up from the outside world, we weren't really exposed to the knowledge and understanding of what took place historically. We didn't know about slavery. We didn't have any black role models.

Strong in our newly discovered knowledge, we pledged to stand tall and proud. And if anyone thought we would stand for any shit, they had better think again. We fought back to back against the police, our dreaded enemy. We stood firm when people tried to belittle us and put us down. Believe it or not, we had just begun to realise we were black. Up until then we just considered ourselves human beings in a world of human beings. But coming here to London, or rather, being released from children's homes, we realised that people related to us as being black. How we were as a person, an individual, didn't really matter. We were 'all the same' as far as most were concerned.

One of the worst things that could be said to us as young guys was 'you people.' "What do you mean by that?" would be the first thing out of our mouths. We realised that society didn't really care much for us and in return we didn't care much for society.

Dave and me were in limbo, disoriented. For essentially we were English, had been brought up as English, but not accepted as English because of the colour of our skin. There began our search to find out who we were and where we really belonged.

The distant lands of Africa and the West Indies were far removed from what we knew. We were at home in the Lyceum, the Palais. We loved shepherd's pie, roast beef, Yorkshire pudding, spotted dick and custard. We went to watch the Spurs play football. We had skinheads, wore Dr Marten's, smooth brogues, Levi's, and Ben Sherman's. We spoke with English accents without a trace or hint of anything else. Our friends were white though we were black, we got on well with them, yet soon realised that we were different. We were English and black, but not accepted as such. We were different from the other black guys. Though they may have been born in Britain, they had deep connections to the West Indies or Africa whereas we had none. They had their own way of speaking interlaced with patois, which we couldn't do.

I remember a few of us went down to a youth club on the Harrow Road. It was called Paddington Youth Club or North Padd. When we got there the guys on the door wouldn't let us in. We must have appeared strange to them. Their excuse for not letting us in was that we were 'white' men. I can tell you that hurt, it really hurt and it nearly kicked off. With our tails between our legs we left. And I will never ever forget.

We went back to the hostel, stood in front of the mirror and practiced our broken English, our patois. We practiced key words and phrases on each other for weeks. We practiced and we practiced, and in the end with many raised eyebrows and not a few smirks, we were finally admitted. And inside those clubs we found something we had never and could never find at the Lyceum, or the Palais, that was an acceptance, a kinship, a warmth, a sense of belonging. But more than that, we had a feeling that we had finally come home.

It was then and there in that club in North Padd, that I looked around, happy, and knew I no longer wanted to be James Bond.

THIRTEEN

Again I was at war with the screws; my one man campaign, and things were coming to a head. The black guy who I was sharing a cell with on basics was a heroin junkie.

"Trevor, they've told me to talk to you, if you don't cool down they're gonna come and do you."

"Fuck 'em and fuck you, what are you, one of them? Don't give me no message from no screw."

He tried to talk to me, but I wasn't having it, and I could see he was nervous because he knew they would be coming.

It was 1997, a few days before Christmas, many of the screws had been drinking and they were up for it. My cell mate had been chasing the dragon most nights. He got his drugs from other inmates on basics. The drugs were transferred from one cell to another by shuttle. This was a sheet of newspaper folded over and flattened with the drug inside. A thick single pipe passed through all the cells which carried heat in winter; in essence it was the radiator. Where it went through to the next cell there was normally a slight space. Placing the shuttle on the pipe it could be slid to the next cell through the gap. At times it was a tight squeeze but with lots of time on your hands it wasn't that hard.

In the beginning, my cell mate's drug taking had been a bone of contention, but in the end we reached a compromise. He was on the top bunk with his head a few inches from the window. So we agreed when he chased his heroin he would put his head at the window and blow the smoke straight out. This wasn't entirely satisfactory to me but it seemed the only realistic option.

I couldn't make him stop, and if you've even been in an enclosed space with a junkie who's going through withdrawals, you know what I mean. They can't sleep, they're forever pacing the cell throughout the night shivering, they become agitated and forever pass wind, spending many hours on the toilet. The smell is as if something had crawled up inside them and died, it was horrendous.

I couldn't ask for a move because they wouldn't move me, not on basics, and they would be happy to know I was suffering some form of discomfort. Anyway nearly every other cell contained someone who was into taking some form of drug. And no way could you come straight out and tell a screw you wanted a move because your cell mate was taking drugs, that was grassing and it wasn't allowed. On normal location some inmates did ask not to be put in with any junkies, but such is the turnover rate of prisoners in Scrubs, it would be virtually impossible not to share the same cell as a junkie at some stage.

One of the ways the screws would detect drug dealers was by the amount of canteen they had. Coming back from the canteen some inmates were loaded down with goodies, obviously some had private cash sent in that they could spend. Routinely the screws would look at your canteen sheet to see if what you had spent tallied with what you had. If it didn't, you had some explaining to do.

Normally phone cards were used as currency to barter for drugs and goods. You were only allowed a certain number of phone cards, any more than that and you were nicked. Those over the limit often passed on cards to others to hold for them and gave them some form of commission. The prison was alive and buzzing with deals going on everywhere; we had our *own* stockmarket and the screws on the outside looking in became more and more frustrated. My cell mate, who I'll call Leo, always seemed able to obtain his gear, whether on the exercise yard or through the shuttle connection; he always copped his stuff.

On Christmas Eve I was involved in several heated altercations with some of the screws from the "firm". The eye-balling, macho preening and the general sizing up of each other was now reaching a critical level and had been steadily building up. It seemed both sides were testing out the other's defensive capabilities before making an all out attack.

At final lock-up, several more than the customary

number of screws appeared at my cell door. The looks they were giving me told me it was time to put my armour on, battle was soon to commence. They slammed the door and went off. After half-an-hour we heard the screws going off duty. For now at least, I was safe. But I knew they would be coming early the next morning. After a while, in that closed environment, you seem to develop a sixth sense.

Several times that night I told Leo that I knew they would be coming in the morning, that his silver foil and other drug gear should be stashed between the cheeks of his arse or thrown away. I impressed upon him that nothing should be found in this cell, for that would be all the excuse they needed to beat me senseless. I am sure without a shadow of a doubt they knew Leo was on the gear. But anything they found they would, of course, pin on me. I told Leo in no uncertain terms, that if any of his paraphernalia or drugs were found in this cell, the responsibility would be his. In other words, he would need to hold his hands up and not put me in it. He agreed to take responsibility.

I knew they had looked up my prison record. Of my seven previous years spent in prison, I had an array of charges, including many assaults on screws. I had been involved in rioting, found guilty of mutiny, inciting others to riot and hitting screws with table legs. The coup-de-grace was handing out Stanley knives while perched atop a barricade marked, "Lets kill the screws." I say I was found guilty, but that's not to say I *was* guilty. They knew my past reputation; I guess that's why it had taken them so long to come for me.

They came at six o'clock Christmas Day. They weren't completely tanked up but by the smell of their breath I knew they had had a few. Of course I had slept on top of my bed— clothes, shoes and all. When they burst in I was sitting on top of my bed, ready for whatever was to come.

"Spin cell search," said Goatee.

I swear I saw some respect in the eyes of some of those evil bastards when they saw that I had been expecting them and was ready. It was a game to them, the thrill of the chase. They were a pack of animals hunting their prey. And it was a good hunt, they had a good adversary. The hunt wasn't to be easy after all, but it was good sport. Tally ho!!

A spin is one of the most stressful parts of prison life because it brings home to you that while in prison you have no privacy. And anything you consider personal is in fact, not so. It also shows you that any rights you have in prison are extremely limited.

The routine for a spin was that you were strip-searched, then told to wait outside while they searched your cell. While doing this they closed the door and went through all your personal belongings: letters from loved ones, personal pictures, everything. It was in some ways poetic justice, for I'm sure many prisoners had gone through other people's private property, especially in the act of burglary.

In most cases during the strip search you were required to squat naked. I say in most cases, because they knew there were a few prisoners, including myself, who would never ever do that and would rather die. I could never understand why anyone did it, because the only person who had that kind of authority was the doctor. But such is the fear of violence, or the loss of remission, that this usually ensured co-operation.

Two screws stood inside the cell with Goatee while three stood outside with Leo. We went through the procedure. First you take off your shoes to be checked, then socks, then shirt which you are allowed to put back on. Trousers and underpants follow. I was not asked to squat. Leo was next and went through the same course of action. After they finished with him they locked us both in the shower room while they searched the cell.

Alone, I asked Leo what he had done with his stuff. His reply so astounded me that that for a minute I didn't believe I had heard right.

"You did what?!"

"I put the foil with a bit of gear on it between the pages of a magazine."

I couldn't believe this guy was so stupid, he had to be setting me up. What the fuck was going on here? One of the first places the screws look for drugs is between the pages of books and magazines. But before I had time to question his motives, the door was flung open by a triumphant Goatee, holding between his fingers a piece of foil with brown/black splotches which were obviously traces of heroin.

Individually, we were called into the office which was next door to the shower room. I was first into the office. Outside, more and more screws appeared, nodding and winking to each another as if to say, "We got the bastard."

"Is this yours, Hercules?"

"No."

"Wait outside."

I stood outside the door, which was open. They brought Leo in.

"Is this yours?"

"No."

Well I couldn't believe what I had just heard, the little shit.

"Right, you're both nicked. Come on."

As we marched past the rows of smiling faces back to our cell, I turned to Leo and said loudly, "You're a piece of shit, you're not even a man."

When we got to the cell door, he didn't want to come in. Instead, he blurted out, "All right then, its mine."

The way he said it was as if he was sacrificing himself, as if I didn't want to admit or own up to my own guilt. I realised this piece of shit was as slippery as an eel, and in a roundabout way he was trying to put me in the frame alongside himself. It was if he was saying, "You know Hercules Governor, he's a nutter, it's not really mine but I'll own up anyway." Implying that he had no option, that if he didn't claim it he would be in trouble with me.

Well you can imagine what kind of Christmas I had in that cell with that toad. No, I didn't do him harm, not that I didn't want to. When I looked at him he was such a pathetic specimen he wasn't even worthy of my energy, so I just ignored him.

The screws knew that those drugs were not mine.When in prison I kept myself extremely fit. I trained in my cell both day and night. The screws knew that the people I associated with were against hard drugs. In the end, Leo was duly charged; I was not. Their plan hadn't worked this time but I knew they would be back again. It was just a matter of time.

ON A WARM SUNNY afternoon I found myself over in Camden town, in a local pub were I knew many of the patrons. At the back they had a beer garden, wonderfully constructed with many over-hanging vines with small brightly coloured flowers. It could have been a scene from the 18th century; it was a throw-back to those days. And I vaguely remember seeing coats of arms adorning the walls of the pub when I had first entered.

The beer was flowing and conversation was good, and there were was many exaggerated stories flying about which caused much amusement and merriment. The company I was in was mixed both black and white, very cosmopolitan as Camden tended to be. A few hours later and several pints consumed, I noticed a tall slender black guy with freckles studying me. I wasn't put off or offended; as his gaze wasn't hostile but more of an inquiry as if he couldn't decide if he might know me. In the end I spoke.

"All right bruv have I seen you somewhere before? I don't know. You seem familiar".

He took his cue.

"I'm sure I saw you in Finsbury Park in a Pub sometime ago, fighting with three guys, you done well blood, the shit was really hitting the fan". Not that I was drunk but I immediately became alert and any semblance of alcohol that was in my head completely disappeared. My whole persona changed to the extent that others at the table asked was I alright as the atmosphere took on slightly tense overtones.

I studied him slowly and intently before I spoke again, and now the table was quiet, because there was no doubt that there was a friction around the table, as sparks were flying from me and everyone around the table knew something was going on. But what?

"Do you know those three guys" I said staring intently into his face, my eye's never leaving his.

People around the table began to shift about uncomfortably because there was no mistaking now, trouble was fast around the corner.

"No! No! I don't know them at all; I was just in the pub when the fight broke out. I don't even know them!!"

"Have you ever seen them before? Do you know where they live? Do you know where they go? Do you know where I can find them?"

The light hearted mood around the table had now gone completely as I stared straight at him. No one else spoke.

All of a sudden the flood-gates opened and from his mouth gushed half gibberish some pleading and some information. The gist of which, was that he had seen them earlier this very same day in a pub opposite Kentish Town Station called The Bull.

"Of course they're not my friends." he stated firmly looking straight at me, and I believed him. He had the look now of a man who had been minding his own business just travelling through the woods, stopped to look at something interesting. 32And was then snared by some trap left for some other predatory animal, and was now in a deep hole looking for a way out.

I gave it to him.

"I believe you".

As I rose from the table I saw and heard him let out a long sigh of tension and relief, and momentarily lifted his eyes heavenwards, no doubt in a silent prayer, because I had turned from companionable drinking buddy nice friendly guy, to a wild eyed crazed interrogator of someone I believed was holding vital information from me; information that I needed immediately. My first thought was to get to that pub opposite Kentish Town station as quickly as possible. But I wanted to diffuse the situation somewhat, and not let on it was as serious as it was. Firstly I don't like people knowing my business, nor did I want anyone marking the bully's card, because perhaps then he'd try and pay me a visit first. I hung around for another fifteen minutes drinking laughing off the incident as nothing special and that it was all forgotten. I'm a good actor, but inside I was seething raging, and what, to know they may have been so close and I was still here not going after them. I could stand it no longer, so I said my goodbyes and took my leave. Unless you knew me you would know where I was going and what I was going to d o, you would know exactly.

"We don't sell single kitchen knives" said the man behind the counter.

"The only ones we have come in a set of four."

"Yes, yes, yes, I'll take that thank you very much, yes that will do nicely."

"Which set would you like sir?"

"The first set, yes the first set that will do."

"What colour"

"Any fucking colour just give me the fucking thing can you please, I'm in a hurry I'm parked on a double yellow line."

Madness was alive and kicking and eager to get on with the business at hand, and he screamed at me get a move on. I ran from the shop to the car faster than any Linford Christie's sprint. And I would have beaten him too.

It was only a five minute drive but it seemed to take an eternity and I'm sure I was stopped by every red light going. My heart was beating so fast I thought it might jump out of my chest, but none of that mattered. I parked around the corner from the pub, but as I headed towards it I thought about my security. But I needn't have worried, because they were not there, but there was something there that brought a huge grin to my face. Clive. I met Clive in prison, and we'd been friends ever since but had lost contact but we were both so happy to meet up again.

"You look good blood" I said to him still smiling.

"For all the tales I've heard about you son I'm surprised you're still standing."

"Well you know me I'm a stubborn bastard I'll be there at the death mate."

His offer of a drink was accepted, though I suggested another pub and we took our leave still laughing and reminiscing about the old days.

We used to get up at six o'clock in the mornings and follow security vans, to check their routines. Clive was a trusted soldier, he was proper, but more than that he was like my own brother. Of course by the time we had reached his house I had told him all about my beef with the bully and his henchmen. Clive smiled, and his eyes twinkled with their old mischief as he looked at me and said,

"I know where we can find, him right now. I know where his woman lives and he stays there all the time. My heart leapt for joy and sang a tune of revenge, hurt and pain, and madness joined in and sang about dead bodies. This was indeed a wonderful day, a most joyous day; I hugged Clive. Thank you brother. Thank you brother. Thank you brother. No matter how much Clive pleaded, I was adamant that this was my mission and my mission alone. "This is personal, it's not business, it's highly personal." good old Clive, he still persisted but in the end, said he knew and understood, and I knew that he really did.

Around 10 o'clock a sumptuous Erykah Badu look-alike walked in with an equally tasty friend. He introduced Erika to me, as the love of his life and who could blame him, WOW! Despite my protests they insisted I stayed the night and, surprise, surprise the friend was also going to spend the night. Sometime around 12 o'clock, all slightly intoxicated, we found ourselves in a mini cab heading for some night-club over north London.

We danced, we laughed, we ordered more drinks and their matchmaking between me and Nefera, Erika's friend seemed to give an extra spark of electricity to the night out.

They kept on leaving us alone together, then urging us to get up and dance with huge smiles on their faces. Both I and Nefera knew what was going on, but what with the heady music and alcohol we didn't care. And at every opportunity Erika would say,

"It's funny that you're both single."

This was enough to set Clive, Nefera and I off with the giggles, while Erika would look on wide eyed and innocent, saying

"What? What? What?"

But we all knew what. Time to go home, we were rowdy and we eventually got a cab back to Kilburn, back to Clive's flat. There followed an awkward silence, as Erika pulled out the double bedded sofa in the front room left sheets and blanket. Then both she and Clive disappeared giggling like two school kids, who had just done the best set-up in the world. I looked at Nefera and she looked at me and then we both burst out laughing, and before I knew it we were both in each others arms kissing passionately.

Marvin Gaye and Diana Ross floated out from the

speakers. Singing "Stop and listen to your heart, Stop and listen to what it's saying". And I did stop and listen to my heart and it shouted and screamed at me. Katie, Katie, Katie. That night Nefera and I slept together, but we didn't have sex.

We talked most of that morning and we knew that we'd become good friends and what possessed me I don't know but I told her about Katie. I don't know, strange as it may seem, I still don't understand women, but this confession seemed to give me many brownie points with Nefera.

She talked about my honesty, and being a real black-man and how in her heart she loved me and we should keep in contact.

We fell asleep in each others arms only to open our eyes around 11 o'clock in the morning to see Clive and Erika standing above us laughing and clapping their hands making lewd comments. We covered our heads and told them to fuck-off which they did, and for some unexplained reason we started kissing again. But we never had sex. But deep down I felt as if I was betraying Katie, and soon I was out of the bed showered and dressed.

And all the while I thought about the bully, that piece of shit. As I looked in the bathroom mirror, I silently mouthed, "I'm coming for you, I'm fucking coming for you."

Clive and Erika were surprised to see me up and dressed, and looked from me to Nefera to ascertain what was going on. But our kiss as I was leaving reassured them that it was all good between us. Erika gave me a big hug and kiss, and made me promise that I'd come to dinner on Monday. Clive walked me out to the car and we spoke, as only soldiers can and it was real we hugged and said our goodbyes. His last words to me were,

"I'm only a phone call away brother, just remember that Yeah."

THE SATURDAY AFTERNOON traffic was heavy and again my thoughts turned to my life and how it was I came to be at this point in my life. As a youngster I kept everything locked up inside, you know all that personal stuff that I felt was embarrassing.

Feelings, emotions, about my family and how I felt about being in children's homes all those feelings I kept under wraps. They, the authorities, the children's homes, as far as it seemed to me, didn't give a hoot for your emotional well being. All they were concerned with was your physical package; they didn't do 'understanding warmth, empathy, emotion' and such like. But if you fucked about they'd kick the granny out of you.

So it was I never really spoke about the woman who gave birth to me, and even now it's hard for me to say that word, mother. So I don't even think of that word or of that person if I can help it. But at certain periods in my life it was unavoidable, and the times I thought about her the more I hated her, there I've said it. I hated my mother, make of it what you will I'm already the bad guy so it doesn't matter to me. And the "man" whose sperm fertilised that woman's egg, the man who I've never set eyes on before. The man who is somewhere out "there" (if still alive) in the deep blue yonder and know he has a son, I hate you too. As the woman who born me tells it (that's if she can ever be believed) he came from America, impregnated her and then went back to whence he came, having never ever seen his child.

Left holding the baby in the fifties and being a black Jamaican woman in London, I know it wasn't easy. I do know that I was given to white, foster parents who lived in Ladbroke Grove/Latimer Road. Nine or so months later, married with her acquired husband in Tow, she came back to collect me. The story, her husband, my so called 'step father' tells is that I refused to go to my biological mother, and clung on for dear life to my foster mother.

It always seemed to be a great source of amusement to him whenever telling the story in later year when I came back and sat talking to him trying to understand and piece my life together.

He was much older than my "mother", and came from West Africa, Sierra Leone on the West coast of Africa.

He was an engineer and had travelled the length and breadth of West Africa as chief engineer of the railway trains. Of those early years I remember nothing. The union between the two brought forth two sisters and a brother for me. A Jamaican and an African even saying it softly and quietly, still had an explosive ring to it. Of course you've guessed it, things took a turn for the worse, and all wasn't happy in the camp.

What the truth is I still don't know, there were claims and counter claims. She claimed he beat her and was having extra marital sex but what is beyond dispute is that she had another son which was undoubtedly not her husband's. He claimed she was messing around with other men. Whatever the truth of the matter, at seven years old along with the woman who bore me and my newly acquired new born baby brother we found ourselves on the streets.

My other brother along with my two sisters stayed with their "real" father in the house and we were on the streets. The story goes that she couldn't cope and put me into care. I went from Kent to Bedford and God knows where else.

My life was just one blur. I never saw my brother and two sisters for many, many, years later, which was a long time, let me tell you. Let me tell you how I met them. Let me tell you how it was that I found them, but in finding them lost a large part of myself – please let me tell you. I need to tell you.

Just then I opened my eyes...sat upright in bed with my back against the headboard and just stared straight ahead. What the time was I had no idea but it was still evening, I was sure of that. Thinking of my 'mother' and younger brother always troubled me, my brother who I hadn't seen for nearly 20 years.

I'm always mildly surprised when others can recall their childhood, and are quite clear of the sequence of events that took place. I, on the other hand, remember my childhood as a blur, a muddled blur that at times didn't make sense at all to me.

I have a memory of being in a convent in Bexhill,, Sussex called Nazareth House. They had moved me yet again from some other place at the age of ten, I was always being moved. Perhaps a year or so on living in Nazareth house, one day it just dawned on me that my younger brother was there too, I don't know how it happened he was just there. Just like magic.

He was always unhappy, he was always crying, and I guess in a way I pushed him to stand up for himself. I remember one day him running to me crying the cleaner's daughter somewhat older than my brother and a bully to boot had hit him. I marched him right back to the girl and made him punch her back, she ran off to her mother and I got beaten for it, but I didn't care.

Even though my brother was only four I told him over and over again that it was only the two of us and we had to stick up for ourselves. And that's why I hated my mother, not for me but for what I saw my younger brother go through, at the hands of evil tyrants who did and acted as they wished, while chanting the name of God.

A year later they moved me to yet another children's home in Bedford, and my brother was left behind with those evil people. I still feel guilty about that but what could I do I was 11-years-old.

My lasting memory of that place is one of those nuns forcing my brother to eat his eggs even though he hated them. He was choking crying and being sick and still they made him eat those eggs poor defenceless child bullied and abused. Just poor defenceless children bullied and abused by those in power, but what could they, we do? Children's homes are a place where I wouldn't send my worst enemy; they are evil places with evil sinister people. Who run them

At the age 17 walking along the Harrow Road, not far from Fernhead Road, I encountered a rather round and bubbly looking black woman. To my astonishment she asked if my mother's name was Claris her reason being "such a strong family resemblance." After confirming that yes, indeed my mother's name was Claris. I then had to explain to her somewhat embarrassingly that no, I didn't know where she was or how to contact her.

Then she nearly stopped my heart, by saying just a few words. "Your brother and sisters live just down the road there with their father," she said pointing in the direction of Ladbroke Grove. After what seemed an eternity I managed to breathe again, while she gave me directions to flesh and blood that was part of myself, my "family".

It seems incredible looking back to that day of 1971, as I stood frozen to the spot as she waved a cheery goodbye before she went on her way. Emotional turmoil springs to mind, as I tried to come to grips with what this lady had just told me. Brother and sisters, did I have another brother and sisters? Yet in the back of mind, in my sub-conscious, somewhere, I knew that this was so. I had travelled the length and breadth of England to different children's homes with my younger brother, who had now been sent to Jamaica by my mother's brother.

Yes I knew I had a younger brother. But another brother and two sisters, it was very hard to take in. You see I had even forgotten they existed; the years in children's homes had clouded my perception of reality. It took me four weeks of anguish before I finally set off to make the journey that would change my life in a way that I could never foresee.

On a cold and windy day in October, I arrived at my brother and sisters house in Ladbroke Grove. Huddled up in my leather jacket, with flared trousers and an air of trepidation, I knocked on the door. Yet I needn't have been so worried for they greeted me with open arms, as such that I was. A long lost brother.

They were good and kind to me and made me feel most welcome and I was overwhelmed by the love that they showed to me. They were honest and open, as families are and should be and I thank them for that. But for me the past life that had led me to here, had left me with doubt uncertainty and most of all a feeling that no one could really love me or would ever really love me and I, in turn didn't know what love was. But I knew that whatever it was, I was afraid of it. Afraid of it because it was confusing, afraid of it because it gave me such weird feelings, afraid of it because I didn't understand it. But most of all because I believed I didn't deserve it. The bond that the three of them had was there for all to see and it made me smile and I was happy.

But what we had in common in being brothers and sisters was soon, in many ways, to be overshadowed by the fact that they were really Africans. They had a different side that was beyond my reach. Living with their father, their family was African orientated, which was completely alien to me and at times quite daunting.

Explaining away your long lost brother, who no, wasn't African, the mother had abandoned him, just left him to fend for himself. The astonishment and incomprehension that showed on their faces led me to seek shelter elsewhere at times. And again I would run away and hide along with my embarrassment, because even though they were my brothers and sisters, in that environment I was an outsider, on the outside looking in.

It was nobody's fault it was just the way things were, and I such a sensitive soul again would take myself off. Their father my step-father even though now divorced from my "mother" was a kindly soul and a good man.

Even though no longer with us, I still miss him. There were many things I would have liked to have said to him as is always the way when someone passes away you care for. But deep down he wasn't my father even though I tried so hard to make it so.

One of my happiest memories is when I and the "chief" my step father went to Sierra Leone in West Africa. That will live long in my memory until the day I die, it was one of the great pleasures of my life. The confusion of being half brothers and sisters was remedied, by me now taking on the guise of an African. It was easier simple less fuss not so awkward, not so many embarrassing questions. It just seemed to happen and the longer it went on the more I got into it and the more the role became my own.

I was now able to speak the African Creole that they spoke to a certain standard and for all intense and purposes just like my brothers and sisters. Of African father and a West Indian mother, but we called ourselves Africans from Sierra Leone. Who happened to be born here. It just came about that way, it just kept moving on a level. And I so wanted to belong to be part of something. Something that was good. Something that made me warm.

But deep down I was living a lie, and in my sub-conscious I knew it, I knew it was wrong to be somebody you're not, but that was the price I guess I was willing to pay to be amongst my brothers and sisters. But inevitably the guilt set in and I struggled as I still struggle to come to terms with my identity of who I am. But that is my problem, the search for who I am and where I belong and I'm still searching. But I have come to terms with the fact that my name is not Hercules but Crook my father's name or Ledwidge my mother's name. Yet Hercules is a name I carry because it's part of me and part of my life and part of wonderful man who was good and kind to me.

I married an African woman so at least my off-spring would have an identity a language and a culture of kings or queens, and a land to call home which I never had, a place I could call HOME.

FOURTEEN

Disillusionment is a terrible thing when it hits you, because all of a sudden you realise it was all for nothing. And that's exactly how I feel. Because I was in limbo searching, I got swept along with causes, and rebellion that seemed to coincide with my search for who I was. Which led me to prison, loss of any real hope of family life or any goal in life that would enhance me to be a better person.

For what I have become now I am ashamed, for I have wasted my god given talents along the road to near self destruction. Which has also left me, though disillusioned and bitter, with no sense of believing in the things that I know are right. And on the brink of just saying fuck-it whatever will be will be and that's not good because when you reach that stage you then become a highly dangerous individual. I never ever want to become that.

But over the years as I, and many like me, stood up and fought against what we believed to be wrong. We fought for change many giving their freedom and lives to a cause they believed in for things to be better, they believed as I believed. Only for certain black people who claim to be middle class, to sell out the rest of the community. Cowards who are paid by the state in good jobs to keep the rest of us down.

Cowards who have never been on a march or demonstration for our rights, who now hold sway over our communities. And they have sold us out taken the money, houses and cars and sold us down the river. But I say to each and every one of you, we will have our day, and we know who you are. You are the "house niggers" of the slave masters but your time will come.

I REACH HOME; sit outside in the car and my mind drifts. We were on the plane heading for Amsterdam; the flight was scheduled for an hour's arrival. The three of us sat with our own silent thoughts, we were all seated in different places but we could feel each others presence.

We had all worked together before, and knew each others mo down to a tee. To say we were good friends would be pushing it a bit, but when it came to work we were a staunch out-fit. It was all one for one and one for all and we never left anybody behind, we prided ourselves on that.

There was tall Clive sweet boy Clive, six two of sinewy muscle and a smile that I had seen disarm many a dark maiden. His complexion was that of smooth coca butter, and if you didn't know better you'd misjudge him at your peril. He was a black belt karate expert. Next there was Jude even though he may have had a girly sounding name; there was nothing girly about Jude. He was about five foot ten with the build of bad boy Mike Tyson, and believe me, given the chance it was not only pigeon necks he'd ring. And then there was me, yours truly, suited and booted with tortoise shell reading glasses looking for all the world like the good guy. Huh!

It was 1994 and I had been given a nice piece of work by a friend of mine who worked in Hatton Gardens. He travelled backwards and forwards across Europe buying and selling diamonds. Oh yeah, and he was a crooked son of a bitch, just as well for us I guess, because he had set up a jewellers in Amsterdam.

We were on our way to relive him of £350,000 worth of diamonds. We had done our homework and even had fake passports, the job was well planned. We touched down at 7:30pm UK time and separately made our way to the safe house; we had not spoken a word to each other since leaving London.

When we reached the dingy flat everything was as it should be, there was nothing out of place. Because there is nothing more guaranteed to freak me out, than things not being the way they should be.

Phase one completed, we settled down with a bottle of Martell and began to go over our plan. I felt giddy and light headed, but you know, I was still focused on the job at hand. We didn't bring any tools of course, and for what we were about to do we didn't need any. The man at this end was well known to me, as I had been to Amsterdam on several occasions, and he was a business man in his own right and was worth a few bob but could keep his mouth shut. But just in case, Jude had a word in his ear, if you know what I mean.

When he came out of the kitchen he looked like he'd seen a ghost and for the rest of the evening refused to look in Jude's direction. I just pretended I didn't even know what was going on, do him good keep him on his toes. We all settled down for the night, as this coup was planned for early morning, 9.30 to be exact and we needed to be fresh and alert.We dressed in silence, each aware of what we needed to do and we were far away from the place that was 'home' to us old blighty.

None of us echoed the thoughts that lay in our subconscious, the thought of doing time in Amsterdam. Our flight out was at 12.30 and everything had to be precise, on the button just like clockwork. The four of us sat in the parked car and again I wondered why this businessman who had lots of money would risk everything for more, I thought 'you greedy bastard'.

The two men came along and pushed the key in the door, we were in a side alley, but there was hardly any activity and I'm sure we had gone virtually unnoticed.

The three of us were out of the car in a flash and bundled those two men through the door as if they were children. It's surprising how strong you can be when you're determined and focussed, to get something you want desperately. Before they could make a sound they were taped and handcuffed and taken into the back. Just like our information had stated, the safe was neither old nor belled up and just one key opened the treasure trove to our goodies. Everything was just like it was supposed to be and isn't it good when a plan comes together.

Back to the airport, boarded the plane, in the air and on our way back to heaven. Of course we didn't have the jewels on us but we did have security – the friend who gave the information was sitting with a friend of ours until we got our money. The businessman left in Amsterdam would fly over that afternoon and both he and his friend would give us £175,000. If for some reason they disappeared, my friend would have to cough up and he knew and accepted that. But all went smoothly and we were all very happy bunnies. Oh! How I love Amsterdam.

ONCE I HAD A dream of Africa— the mother country, the homeland, where black people came from, where my ancestors came from.

Unlike a lot of the black guys I saw running after white women, I wanted a black woman, a black queen, a Nubian princess. We'd build a wonderful nation of children with a pride, a respect and a love of who they were. It wasn't that I didn't like white women, all women are women, good and bad, regardless of race or creed. But society had forced my hand because it held up white beauty as the pinnacle of desire– blonde hair, blue eyes, straight nose and hair, but most of all, white skin. Everywhere I turned I saw this standard portrayed to an extent that even black people began to believe it.

But I wasn't going to let this society brainwash me into believing that black women and black men were second best. I was a proud young black man, and I wanted a proud black woman who knew who she was, knew her culture. I felt I was fighting a constant battle to establish who I was, to build some self-respect and pride for myself in a society that didn't really understand black people, they hadn't taken the time, didn't want to and maybe didn't know how to. So I dreamt of going to a place I had never been, but looked upon as my home.

That some Africans had a negative attitude toward black people not born there did not deter me. Many times I had heard them call us sons of slaves. I couldn't have cared less, they did not have a monopoly on Africa. Black people in the West Indies, South America, North America and in many cases Europe, were taken to these places in chains, as slaves; we did not choose to go. Africa is our homeland. And Africa was where I wanted to be.

I wanted to marry an African woman so that my children could have a culture, a language and home, and an African name. I wanted them to be able to belong. I wanted them to have their own true history, kings and queens, their *own* heroes. Not like James Bond, or the history that I was taught of King Henry and King James, who had no relationship to me.

I loved Africa; it was the woman that I was looking

for. I loved her completely. I would have done nearly anything for her. She was my queen, she made me feel proud, I would have protected her with my life.

In the old days, before I fell out of love with Africa, I used to dream of myself as a hero, the good guy. And when I was troubled or vexed I would close my eyes and dream of her. I would dream I was a freedom fighter, fighting to liberate South Africa. And so I lay down and dreamt of being a freedom fighter.....

Thursday May 25, 1982
Somewhere in the deep bush of Namibia

My dearest darling,

I don't know how or when you will receive this letter, but I pray it reaches you as do the several others I have sent to you over the past nine months. Joining the Military Freedom Movement in the pursuit of a free South Africa is not what I thought it would be at all. And God forgive me; no, God forgive us, for the things we do in the name of Freedom. If you could see me now I doubt very much you would know me. It is not that I have changed that much in the four years since we have been apart, it is just that there is a cold, hard, menacing, and dare I say, wickedness that surrounds my aura. I can almost feel it physically, it is as if there is one Trevor, the Trevor you used to know, and another Trevor, the cold-blooded kill.... There, I nearly said it, the word I have come to loathe and hate and tried so many times to disassociate myself from, but still it sticks to me clinging with the foul stench of death that surrounds me. I don't know where or when it will end.

Even though we are no longer together, we know that we love each other deeply. I have no one to turn to here nor anywhere else in the world darling, for you are all that has been kind, good, and sweet in my life, and loyal, oh, ever so loyal. If only I could turn back the hands of time I would never have let you go. So it is to you, Sonia, that I pour out my innermost feelings as if you were my confessor. And as always, you are there when I need you. I don't know if or when I will ever see

you again, but you know I love you, I'll always love you. Even though I haven't asked how you are and so many other questions I'd like to ask, you know deep in my heart I do. But such is our bond I know you will know that this letter was just me talking to myself.
All my love and more,
Trevor

As I stood to attention in line with the other soldiers out in the open bush, the Sergeant barked out orders as the men listened intently. We were about to go on some secret mission and as usual the briefing was given in Swahili, which, aside from general military commands, I had not yet mastered. Mack, an American who was next to me staring wide-eyed at the Sergeant, nodded his head ever so slightly at the words being said. He would translate for me later on. "Abeginoishe!" shouted the Sergeant, which meant stand at ease. I did so, in unison with the others.

The Sergeant was still speaking as the men fidgeted. As they did, I tried to gauge their faces and suss out what type of mood they were in, an indication of what our mission might be. Even though I had been on several missions, I was still apprehensive and my palms and the back of my neck began to sweat profusely and my mouth became dry. I could only think, *what would death be like?* And no matter how I tried to shake this thought from my mind, I could not until the mission was over and I was back safely.

I turned to look at Mack, his head nodding became more vigorous and a ghost of a smile touched his lips. I knew then that the action would be serious. "Damn Motherf*****. Right too!" said Mack aloud as the Sergeant glared at him. At last he had finished talking and as the sun gently declined we began loading ourselves into the truck. As we took off into the darkening night I turned to Mack as he said, "We're gonna kick ass brother!" Our orders were to destroy a lookout post near the South African border which I knew from past experience was highly dangerous.

I surveyed the other eighteen soldiers. Some quietly chatted and smoked, while alone others contemplated the events to come or just wondered what the hell they were doing there. They were all African except for Mack and myself and none spoke English. I wondered how it was that I, a so-called 'black cockney', had found myself travelling through a war zone with my African brothers and an American bro', and heading steadily into the darkening night. I was a million miles away from what I knew.

Unhappy in society, my soul had cried daily. I felt uncomfortable. A life of crime and prison became an inevitability and madness was driving me to do all kinds of foolishness and harm in my own community. When a man popped up out of the woodwork and gave me a number to ring, wheels were put in motion. Plane ticket handed to me, met at the airport, and the freedom fighting began. As for the man who came out of the woodwork, he disappeared as a ghost in the night.

Humble thanks was said for helping to come and liberate "our lovely and wonderful country" and toasts all round. Promises of land forever for my children and my children's children were pledged 'on the glorious day of liberation.' And here I was, stomach churning, palms sweaty, unsure of what was to come and afraid.

At last, the truck came to a halt. The soldiers slipped out from the back and into the warm dark night—crouching, guns ready, ears alert. The AK-47 felt unusually heavy tonight as did my breathing. Again, I wondered what the fuck I was doing here.

Now it was time to go. Everyone knew their orders and the group split into groups of five and I stuck close to Mack. Mack was from New Orleans and had come to be like an older brother to me. He sort of adopted me, which I didn't mind because he was so bloody funny. At forty years old he stood about six foot and had slight speckles of grey in his hair. He had a kindness and a love for mankind that can only come from some overwhelming life experience.

The five in our group ran to the electric wire fence. We didn't touch it, for to do so would have meant certain death. My heart was pounding, as we began to dig a hole under the fence. When enough earth had been cleared, one by one we crawled under and over to the the other side. The ammunition dump in front of us was our target, but we had been seen and all hell broke loose. Blam, blam, blam, blam, blam, blam, blam, blam, whoosh, putt, putt, putt, blam, blam, blam. I fired into the night at I know not what.

"Let's go!" shouted Mack who was the explosives expert; but it seemed suicide. Surely we should turn back, but there was Mack out in front and the four of us followed, though I am sure we wanted to turn and go the other way. What happened during those confused moments I can't remember, but the ammunition dump was blown up so our attack had been successful.

We lost five men on that mission and Mack was one of them. He had stayed behind to make sure that the detonator went off. A part of me died with Mack that night and when we got back to camp I sat in the dust cradling my rifle and cried like a baby. The sergeant along with two of the lads brought me over a bottle of palm wine and left me alone, which I thought was a great gesture. I toasted Mack and his family and friends and anybody who knew him. In my drunken state I then toasted my comrades at arms and they themselves got drunk for their comrades, our comrades, comrades who had died for a cause we believed in. And with my gun in one hand the bottle in the other, I looked heavenwards and shouted, "Hey Mack, hey Mack you old bastard, just tell me what will death be like." I knelt down, then pitched forward onto my face and was out for the count.

Friday, August 4/85
Somewhere in the deep bush in Namibia

My dearest darling,

I suppose you've heard the news by now; S. Africa (Azania) is at last free and 'one man - one vote' is at this very moment now being implemented in the Country's first free election since the colonialists and imperialists seized power. I know you have never been as politically minded or motivated as I have and I know you can't understand why I smashed several televisions in my rage (one of which was yours) when I saw women and children being shot down in their own country like dogs.You used to say, "There's no need for that and besides what can we do?"

Well I did something, and in my own small way feel I have contributed to the freedom and rebirth of a nation. I know you disagree with the way I went about it and the methods of guerrilla warfare, but I won't argue the point because you have your views and I have mine. But knowing you, I'm sure you'll rejoice with the rest of the world at the freedom of a people who were oppressed in their own country simply and solely because of the colour of their skin.

I feel euphoric, yet I'm still saddened by the death of Mack; remember the American I wrote you about? Oh, what a rejoicing we would have shared on such a glorious day as this; he was a true hero and I promise to erect a statue of him as soon as possible. Incidentally, I am to be honoured along with my comrades today, by no less than the chiefs and leaders of all the political parties who opposed apartheid. I'm told it's the highest honour anyone can receive and for the first time in my life I've gained some recognition. I know it may not be the type of recognition you'd want for me, but I believed in the cause. I didn't do it for money or any personal gain but because I believed; always remember that I believed.

The hot sun is making me thirsty and I need to go and change for the ceremony this afternoon, so I'll end this letter. I don't know when or if I'll ever see you again; I hope so. Remember I'll always love you, but here in Azania I have found another love, and it may seem strange when I tell you it is the love of life.

All my love,

Trevor
xxxx

The platform was raised high, and below us at least a hundred thousand people clapped and cheered when our names were called out. I was on the platform along with my comrades from the military freedom movement. I had never felt such heady joy in all my life. Myself and my comrades hugged each other with tears in our eyes as we each individually walked along the platform to receive our medals. When I went to receive mine I was hugged by tearful leaders as I was given a medal and a rolled parchment. I was given Mack's medal and parchment to pass on to his next of kin. All around me people hugged each other with tears of joy. Any misgivings I may have had about joining the freedom movement and what I had participated in were wholly and completely dispelled.

One of my comrades in the military movement invited me back to his place along with his two brothers and sisters. We were greeted by what seemed like the whole town; everybody admired our medals. The parchment disclosed that we had been given land and enough money to set up home wherever we chose.

I took the jeep to go off on my own and stopped at a nearby bar. I drank to Mack and his memory then cursed him for deserting me and then drank to Mack some more. As nightfall came I staggered from the bar hardly seeing, and bumping into people outside who then started to wag their fingers and chastise me for being drunk. Suddenly Zenga's brother, who had been sent to look for me, was at my side explaining that I was one of the Military Movement. Everybody's attitude changed and they hugged me and the women kissed my cheeks and not for the first time that day I was overwhelmed with love.

I looked towards the heavens and I shouted, "Mack you old bastard, you old bastard, what's happening man? I've got your stuff or as you'd say, your *thangs*. We're heroes brother, we're heroes, Mack you son of a bitch." As I was led to the jeep by Zenga's brother I turned and shouted to the sky, "Mack, what is death like? Tell me you bastard, tell me what will death be like."

STILL HAUNTED BY the fact that I was back in prison again, I wondered: Was this forever to be my way of life, had I become so numb to prison that I now accepted that it would always be part of my existence? If so, what would I look forward to next time– ten years, twenty years, life?

I put down the book I was reading; my whole body broke out into a cold sweat as I sat down on my bed. Was my life so precariously balanced that it seemed I had no control over it? What happened to my free will? What happened to defining my own life, and what's more what had happened to my brain? Madness screamed out at me, "You're a fucking warrior, don't you understand? You're a fucking warrior, no retreat, no surrender."

Madness had, from the earliest days, been in the background pushing, urging me forward to the front line. Along with my anger it had teamed up to help me fight the real or imaginary injustices that I believed were inflicted on me. Together we stood firm, we were one. And when all the others were selling out we stood solid, fuck the consequences. We'd never put 'make-up' on to hide who we were, we were black and proud and would always be.

FIFTEEN

As I approached my cell, there he was again, using me as a barometer for his masculinity. It was dinner time, I was still on basics and had just gotten my meal. But this ginger-headed screw - who I knew to be on steroids - had recently taken to standing outside my door as soon as he saw me coming towards it. If you pushed me and asked me what he was about, I would say that he was a frustrated closet gay. Frustrated at being in such a macho environment where to "come out" would be suicide. Anyway, he had taken to standing outside my door and taking his time to open it, playing games like a little child. Mind games. I tried to ignore him because, he was what we would call a "bulla man". He was the type of man who would get pleasure from confrontation, especially rolling about on the ground with you. He definitely was a "bulla man". Most times I had just ignored him. But not today. Madness that sometimes crept up on me when I felt that people were taking the piss, was ready for.....whatever.

There he was, key in the door, fiddling about and looking at me with that sick smile on his face. By the time I got there he was still fiddling with the cell door, looking at me. "Yah! I kicked the door as hard I could and as it flew open, I promptly walked in. He stood at the doorway looking at me, gone was his sick smile, to be replaced by frustration and temper. "You keep pushing it Hercules, you're gonna get what's coming to you."

"Yeah, Yeah, Yeah." Madness had gripped me and taken over and it was his turn now. Blam! I kicked the door shut. "Who gives a fuck," Madness said, "we're all gonna die someday, it's *how* you die." I had to agree. "But no screaming like a bitch Trev," said Madness laughing. I loved him. When the door opened a few seconds later, Leo came in, nervous as fuck saying, "They've told me to get my kit and move to another cell."

As Leo packed his kit, Ginger was smiling smugly at me. In other words he was relaying to me indirectly that they would be coming. Madness was in his element. He somehow made me tear off my shirt and start shadow boxing– grunts groans, and all. And Madness kept repeating, "It's a good day to die." I agreed, and not for the first time I realised I might be just as mad as Madness. Leo couldn't wait to get out and who could blame him.

I knew and understood Madness, he was a freedom fighter and so was I. It was like fighting for your country, your land and family. Fighting for what's right, fighting for what belongs to you. You are prepared to die for it and that's how I felt at times. After all, hadn't I dreamt of going to Angola to fight against the oppressor? Hadn't I wanted to go to S. Africa to fight with the A.N.C.? More than anything in the world I wanted to be a hero, to be somebody. I wanted respect and I wanted people to respect me. I wanted to go down in history and for people to write about me; I wanted to be a hero for my children, and their children's children.

As I shadowboxed the tears flowed down my cheeks. I cried with happiness and I cried with pride. I would never ever be intimidated, I would rather die. By this time Ginger had gone. Gone to tell the rest that they were dealing with a madman. A madman driven on by a desire and a will they did not and could not understand.

After about half-an-hour they still hadn't come, so I sat down and ate my dinner. Nearly one hour had passed since Ginger had left and still nothing. The cells were due to be opened in about ten minutes and so I assumed they would not be coming. How wrong I was. I went over to the toilet in the corner of the cell, pulled my trousers down and sat down on the basin. No sooner had I sat down than the door flew open and they poured in and poured in. The next thing I recall I was lying face down on the floor and they were trying to get the cuffs on me. A few of them were punching me but that soon stopped. All I could hear was a voice saying, "Don't struggle, we're not gonna hurt you, we're just taking you down the block."

I couldn't breathe, someone had me in a choke hold. All of a sudden a black screw - a Muslim brother - appeared and said, "Let him go, he can't breathe." I guess he thought that should buy him some brotherhood points, but to me he was just the same as the rest. They had dragged and beaten inmates black *and* white, and no screws had tried to intervene.

Literally I was dragged off to the block. I would really like to say I kicked some serious butt, but I didn't. I was hog tied and bounced down those iron stairs all the way into the block, where I was handed over to the block screws and duly locked up. I wasn't too badly shaken up, I had scrapes and bruises on my arms and the inside of my bottom lip was bleeding but apart from that I guess I was fine.

I went in front of the Governor, in fact it was one of the Deputy Governors, a lady. She knew who I was and I knew who she was. We'd both done a TV programme for BBC 2 and she was one of the people sitting around the table. Then she was an ordinary screw, but had since risen to the position of Deputy Governor. When I came in she asked if the lady who was present could stay, she was a member of the Board of Visitors. I said, "Yes."

I had been charged with assault, although my cell door should have been locked and no screws should have been in my cell at the time. The Deputy Governor looked daggers at the officer, the abuse was apparent and she could see I had been manhandled. I was eager to hear the Senior Officer's explanation.

I plead not guilty. The SO began to read out his evidence and the more he read, the madder and more red-faced the Deputy Governor became. It was obvious to anyone that the whole concoction was a tissue of lies. And when she asked if he had any witnesses, he said, "No." What a fucking mug, no one would even come and give evidence for him.

In the old days you would never ever be found innocent if you were charged with assaulting a screw. But as I watched this scene unfold in front of me it became clear that this brutality had been going on for some time and it appeared the Deputy Governor had had enough. Several times she asked me if I was all right. I replied, "Yes," but my disgust for the officer in front of her was obvious for all to see.

When she asked me to reply to the officer's accusations I replied, "Well Miss, I was sitting on the toilet when they burst into the cell." She asked the officer if this was true. The silly bastard replied, "Yes." Her face reddened considerably. "Also Miss, when they dragged me down the block, my trousers were around my legs." She looked up with a face of thunder, "Is that true?" "Er, er, er, yes Mam." Silly bastard. She took one minute to write something down then she said, "I find no charge to answer."

Now let me tell you, in all my time in jail I have never heard the likes of this. I have heard "guilty," "not guilty," or "benefit of the doubt," but never ever have I ever heard "no charge to answer."

For the first time since I had come back to prison, I realised some fundamental things had changed. As I stared ahead watching the Deputy Governor write notes in her book, my thoughts drifted. I was brought back to the present as the screw tapped me on the shoulder and said, "Lets go."

Outside the Governor's office, one of the block screws told me they would be taking me back to the wing. I replied, "No, I'm staying down the block." This, as you can imagine, caused some consternation and they brought me into the office. Once in the office they offered me tea, I declined. We talked about how things in the prison service had changed over the years. They knew I, like them, was of the old school of "them and us" and I was having difficulty coming to terms with us all being pally.

I explained that the accusing officer had just been called a liar and had been embarrassed beyond belief. As I was already having grief up there on the wing, what was my life likely to be worth now? To my surprise, the screw asked if he sorted it all out would I go back then? I was dubious at first, but I realised that this man carried a lot of power and so I agreed. Off he went and twenty minutes later he reappeared and said, "Sorted." You could see he felt quite chuffed with himself as if to say to me, there you are son, I have got power.

The two block screws took me back to the wing. On the two's, in the office, we talked to Goatee and several of his friends. I could not believe how contrite they were. Whether it was because their boss had failed so miserably, I don't know. But I do know I saw them for what they were: bullying scum. We agreed a truce and I was taken off basics. After that, a lot of the times my door was left open and I could usually nip down and get a shower. Soon afterwards, I was moved to Wandsworth and then Elmley.

Not long after I reached Elmley I heard that about twenty prison officers from Wormwood Scrubs had been charged with numerous assaults on prisoners. I cheered along with the others and as I looked heavenwards I shouted aloud, "Thank you God, Thank you God!"

SIXTEEN

It was late evening and the sun was high in the sky. Birds all about chirped and sang happily, refusing to go to roost until the last minute. It was wonderfully hot but not humid, with a sexy, gentle breeze that just caresses you every now and then just to let you know life was good.

I climbed upon the re-plated stolen motorbike, donned my helmet, eased the bike into first gear and headed into the steady flow of south London traffic. I was attired in grey, trying to be as nondescript as possible; my gloves were black and woollen. As I rode, the breeze gently wrapped its arms around me. I could have been on the high seas sailing, and I pictured myself standing on the front of a yacht as it glided through the open sea.

The traffic was quite heavy but on the motorbike it made no difference; easily I could by-pass slow moving vehicles. I was conscious of the gun in my pocket and I resented it being there. It seemed clumsy, awkward, heavy; like an out of control party guest that you couldn't make leave. You were at their mercy, but once you got rid of them you would say never again. But first, you had to get rid of them.

I blanked my mind and rode freely in the sexy breeze, allowing it to take my hand and guide me through its undulating highs and lows. I had done my homework and I knew exactly where the bully would be. Today there would be no mistakes, blunders, or miscalculations. No misjudgements, oversights, slip-ups— none of these. Today would be the day.

Opening up the throttle slightly, I headed towards my date with destiny. In an instant, it turned cold. As I pulled up, there he was as I knew he would be, sitting on his girlfriend's wall. There was no mistaking him. He was alone and acted as if he didn't have a care in the world and I was determined to make that a reality. He didn't know what was coming as I walked down the street towards him— helmet on, both hands in my pockets and my right hand finger curled around the trigger of the gun.

I came within five feet of him. He looked up but didn't move. I pulled out the gun, pointed it at his head and said softly, "God forgive me."

Elmley Prison was a daunting place because everything seemed so enclosed, so claustrophobic. You felt hemmed in. It was like being stuck on an underground carriage and unable to move into the next car.

I tried as best as I could to avoid trouble here and for the most part I was successful. I used the gym nearly every day for the weights, and ran round the track in the mornings to rid myself of my frustrations. On the odd occasion I would play football but not that often. In this macho environment there was the incentive to try and prove your manliness, to be competitive, but I had been through all that shit before and believe me I didn't need it. I had nothing to prove.

Life in Elmley began to run on an even keel for me and that suited me just fine. The letters I recall from an old flame, who was now in America, helped a lot too and made me feel so good. And if your reading this Polly, you are wonderful, you are special and you'll always have a place in my heart until the day I die.

Eventually they moved me to house block five, which was the top privilege one could acquire there. Within weeks of arriving on block five, the rumours that each cell was to be given a portable TV turned out to be a reality. There were two men per cell, but now there were two men per cell plus colour television. The world had gone mad.

For the first few weeks people stumbled out of their beds, eyes barely open through lack of sleep. It was truly amazing. Things had certainly changed since my day. Now there were women screws, pay phones that could be used to ring home *and* colour TV's. But one thing I can tell you, it brings home that nothing can compensate for your loss of freedom.

Not long after, I was told I would be moving to

Stanford Hill. Stanford Hill was an open prison and it meant I would soon be on my way out. For someone like me who had only ever been in enclosed prisons, Stanford Hill would be like a breath of fresh air, if that could ever really be said of any jail.

About eight if us who had been given D-category status set off in a mini bus to Stanford Hill. Stanford Hill is literally 800 yards from Elmley. Both prisons are in Kent Sheerness on the isle of Sheppy. There is also a third prison called Swale side, which is maximum security and all three are in sight of each other and surrounded by green open spaces.

When we arrived at reception we were not surrounded by authoritarian screws barking out orders, but by two inmates who were formerly at Elmley who told us to relax, that it's good here. Usually when you come into a prison's reception it's quite daunting and at times unpleasant because the screws want you to be in no doubt as to who's in charge. One screw processed us through reception. The atmosphere there was cordial and there was an air of openness. But what struck me the most was the courteous and pleasant manner of the screws who met us in the reception area.

Stanford Hill had two main wings: A and B. These buildings where situated in the middle of an open plan complex consisting of dining hall, gym and swimming pool. Yes that's right, Stanford Hill had a swimming pool. I couldn't believe it at first, but take my word for it, when they said it was an open prison, they meant just that, an open prison. There was no high, forbidding wall; there was no barbed wire fence. In fact there was no fence at all as far as I could make out. It seemed that if you took it upon yourself to escape you could virtually walk out unopposed. In other prisons, everywhere you go you were normally escorted by a screw, but here you were allowed to move about the outside of the main wings unaccompanied. As I said, it was like a breath of fresh air. Flowerbeds of wonderfully exotic flowers surrounded the buildings. Prison officers, prisoners, and staff all strolled around and mixed freely.

Many may consider Stanford Hill to be unreasonably cushy. But in fact, when you think about it, we prisoners had to come back into society. And without a shadow of a doubt I can say that it was a healthy and constructive way to ease the transition. All the instincts I had for self-preservation and the predatory posturing of being in a male dominated enclosed environment seemed to ebb away as each day passed. The fact that I was treated as a human being played no small part in the fact that I only once got into trouble during my eight months there. But at the end of the day, prison is prison, and you are denied your freedom and are locked away from those you love and care about.

Life went on. I worked as a cleaner on the wing and was usually finished within an hour as long as I kept my head down and I was left to my own devices. I had developed a taste for backgammon, which I had learnt in Elmley at the expense of numerous phone cards. Nearly every hour I had space, I played with Mal, who nicknamed himself the white hunter and was a real joker. He was very good, but I swear he tampered and fixed the dice and when I wasn't looking, moved pieces on the board. How else could he have beaten me?

I'm sorry to say that my dice often fell victim to my frustration at losing. It got so bad one day that I threw the dice across the board so hard that they bounced and flew back only to land at my feet. Our games were animated and fascinating; compulsory viewing. At times the cell was bulging with eager inmates waiting for an eruption and dice to go flying. I do wish to say though, it was all done tongue and cheek and we were, and still are, friends. But Mal, I'm sure you cheated me son. And wipe that smug smile off your face.

As the years had passed, I longed and yearned to be a normal person with a home, family, something to belong to. I was tired of fighting a struggle that many black people had now abandoned. I was an old warrior, things had changed, moved on. It wasn't the seventies or eighties, it was the nineties, a different time. I was tired of confrontation, I was tired of believing that I had to challenge every little thing said or done to me, in the name of the race.

As I looked around at black people in this society, I realised many of them were happy at the way things were. They weren't struggling for political change, they were happy to let someone else fight their battles as they sat back and reaped the benefit of those who did struggle and fight. I thought back to the Brixton riots and my heart saddened at those protesters who were beaten and flung into vans, carted off to police stations, taken to court and sentenced to prison. Sentenced for rebelling for what they believed to be wrong. For the most part they were unemployed or on the lower rungs of the ladder of this so called society.

Their defiance wasn't in vain. Society had stood up and taken notice of these angry people and went some way to pacify them. Society created some meaningful jobs for black people and created laws against discrimination. Soon you could find black people in positions of power. But let me tell you, most of those black people have never made any defiant gestures to win their prized positions. Many of those black people who were given good jobs did so on the strength of our rebellious convictions. But don't worry, their time will come and they will be exposed and seen for what they are: "house niggers," to keep the rest of us down.

SEVENTEEN

I couldn't do it; for the life of me, I just couldn't do it. He sat there on the wall, rigid with fear, staring at me. It seemed he wanted to say something but no words or sounds were forthcoming. I said not one word; but stared through my visor at the man in front of me. A sudden thought flashed through my mind. I was now the bully, and I was perpetuating a cycle of violence in which the *most* violent man would be declared the winner, the man. That was very disturbing, and went against everything I've ever believed. How did I ever reach this point? How did I get here? Had my life been so cruel and turbulent that I should find myself standing here ready to do such a deed? Could it be genetic?

I looked at him. He was pathetic. He wasn't a bad man, he was a bully and a coward. He was mouthing "Please, please, please," but still words couldn't come out. I backed away several feet, put the gun in my pocket, turned and briskly walked away. Around the corner, the bike started instantly and I was soon in the evening traffic. I felt a glorious weight had been lifted from my shoulders; everywhere it seemed there was a song. The whole city looked as I had never seen it before— magnificent, spectacular, splendid. And the more I rode on, my heart jumped and leaped with happiness and joy.

Thank you Lord. There but for the grace of God.... I knew this was a turning point in my life, I just knew it. What I had intended to do was wrong, very wrong, very wrong indeed. Not only was it wrong within the macho world of violence; it was wrong for me, not right for *me*. I still had morals and values and a love of life. And I could still differentiate between wrong and right and I did believe in God.

I rode into the clearing, parked the bike, walked under the bridge and stopped. It was quite dark now but the huge river in front of me reminded me of a song about the Mississippi by Paul Robeson. That it *'keep rolling along.'* I took the gun and the bag of bullets and threw them as far as I could into the river. I stood there for several minutes, as if cleansing myself, and then offered a prayer. *Thank you Lord*. My life could never be the same again, of that I was sure. I wanted my life back, and I now understood that you could get your life back, that you could change. And believe me, I *would* change.

As I climbed up on the motorbike and rode away, I felt an intense sense of tranquillity, such that I have never experienced before. And I knew then that I would be okay. As for Katie, we went our separate ways but remained good friends. As far as relationships go, I still had issues that needed to be resolved and I know that it will take time.

Many months later I heard through the grapevine that the bully had died. He collapsed and died of a heart attack. And I couldn't help but think back to the dream I had. Vengeance is Mine!!

NOWADAYS THINGS HAVE changed; it's not like the old days. Society, the world has moved on. People's attitudes have hardened and it has now become SELF, ME, I want, I need, I have to have it. NOW! You're no longer judged on who you are but what you've acquired, as long as you have it.

The countries with the most fire power, the biggest armies, and the most leather weapons claim all kind of nonsense about other weaker countries just to go to war with them. To bully and dictate and take what they want for their own greed and their secret agendas, regardless of the innocent lives it cost, who cares? But there is no justice for the families and friend who lives mean nothing to those who have taken them or they make the rules, they alone are judge and jury in whatever they do, because they are right because they have might. And so those who are truly and undoubtedly wronged take matters into their own hands and more confusion then begins to reign. And so all over the world people are seeking revenge and revenge for past and present misdemeanours. Or seeking compensation or an apology, while others are just trying to feather their own nests on the strength of some misfortune, mishap or atrocity that has taken place. And along come the opportunists and vultures seeking to make gain and profit from others misfortune, hurt, pain and loss.

While the world society then becomes divided into those who are for or against, and those who believe they have been wronged, victimised, alienated, marginalised. Even though they may not be politically active or aware, deep within they harbour some deep rooted resentment and in many cases HATE. And the chilling thing is they BELIEVE it.

Whether you agree or not depends on which side of the fence you're on, or the side of the fence life has dealt you. But there is no doubt the world is segregated, society is segregated and unfair, and you either live with it the way things are, especially if things are alright with you, you don't open your mouth, you don't make a fuss. But there are others whose consciousness led them to rebel, in what ever form that may be or take.

I guess in that case you could say I was a rebel. In the fact that ever since I left school, and the way I've been treated and humiliated just due to the colour of my skin. Yes, this has made me a rebel. And the more I found out and learned, the more I could see the everyday liberties being taken with me and other black people here and all across the world, and it made me angry and frustrated.

Yes! I guess many people would say I have a chip on my shoulder. As I said it depends on what view you take, because to me I was a confused youngster looking and searching for who I was my identity in a society that didn't represent me. I was eager to find out like everybody else where I belonged in the scheme of things.

When I did find out, I wasn't very happy and to me it was all so unfair. Yet, there were others like me growing up in this society in the late sixties and seventies who felt the same way. Every time we saw and heard people like Alf Garnett shouting and screaming "wogs", ? and "jungle bunnies" from our TV screens, our sense of injustice raised another notch and the fire raged within us, burning a deep anger into our souls. And when we saw pictures of the brutality taking place against black people in South Africa while the rest of the world looked on.

That anger and frustration boiled over into a RAGE WITHIN, that could only at times be described as self-destructive. As we now took on attitudes and stances of aggression and a fire in our bellies that at times we weren't able to control.

We lashed out at everything and everyone and even at each other in our confused and angry state. But most of all we blamed this society, for colonialism and imperialism and worst of all slavery. We even began to find insult and disrespect in the most innocent greetings or pleasantries.

"Hello, sunshine" was guaranteed to set us off foaming at the mouth, ready to bite any mother fucker's head off, who we thought were talking to us like some pickaninny. Things just seemed to escalate until we were finally on the outside looking in. It was as if we believed we were alienated, or we just alienated ourselves – that wasn't the issue to us. The fact of the matter was that we were on the outside and knew we were different. Most of us were teenagers with no proper guidance- fathers or role models to set us off in the right direction, on the rocky road called life.

We went in search of our identity and of who we were in a society that was white that did not reflect us or our views and of course the first question we asked ourselves was how it was that we came to be here, in a place we felt we didn't belong or a place that we believed didn't really want us but just tolerated us.

Most white teenagers with good families in a society that they were at ease in, still had to go through their confusion of who they were and their place in life. I'm not making excuses but imagine what it was like for us, at times I didn't know whether I was coming or going.

Most of us with no families or homes soon found ourselves on the streets because the hostels and other such institutions we found ourselves in soon didn't want us, nor could they cope with this new generation of brash arrogant black youngsters.

We were a challenge and we challenged anything and everything and anyone that didn't agree with our point of view. We became isolated from the normal everyday members of our society, that went about their normal legal business. We found and joined with those regardless of skin or creed who also had become isolated or alienated for whatever cause. We formed and bonded together and pointed our accusing fingers at those who we believed to be our oppressors and enemies. The anger and frustration just continued into adult life.

Time to move on

I've been at war for as long as I can remember against a society that I believed alienated me and didn't want me. A white society into which I was born, where I felt I should have been treated with equality, and afforded a respect. That as I grew up I saw was denied to me, and others of a similar ilk to myself.

I rebelled, I fought vociferated my grievances and stood firm against my understood oppressor. And even spent many years in jail disrupting and harassing the system, on my crusade for respect and my identity. In the name of "pay-back" was my justification for anything or if anything that I did, that would somehow touch my conscience which I knew wasn't right. That which was wrong.

Through-out it all I was fighting for a cause I believed in. A cause that I should stand up for my blackness since the sixties from people like Alf Garnett who appeared on our T.V. screens in comedy shows shouting out "black bastards coons wogs jungle bunnies" to the hurtful laughter of the audience that filled my ears. Followed by the taunts on the school playground the following day.

Then there were the history lessons of black savages deep in the jungle, and of slaves. It was portrayed to me that this was my only history, and that of colonialism, and I cried when I watched them killing young children in South Africa because of the colour of their skin.

And here I was in England supposedly English, as I watched this country's government play its part in that oppression while at the same time it was made clear to me that I was no different than any other black, they called wog or coon.

But as the years passed my rebellion and good intentions that I once had now took on a criminal element and I along the way became no better than a common criminal, much to my dismay. Looking back now I'm ashamed to say that I lost the plot, lost my direction, and the things I understood to be good, and the fight for justice for all fell by the way-side.

Yet now it seems funny that, that Africanness I once craved and longed for to be accepted is no longer that important to me. In fact I shy away from that now, because I am international, universal a member of the human race I at long last happy with who and what I am, and that is me Trevor Hercules Ledwidge.

I and others like me spent years in jail sticking up for what we believed to be the rights of black people. Enabling others to come here to a society that has changed in many ways for the better for black people. And the" WAR" that I and many others waged back in-the-day is no longer that relevant. And those of us who fought and struggled to bring an awareness and consciousness, both to ourselves and others, now look on as people from other continents now arrive. Yet they are still immersed in colonialism and view us the old guard with somewhat of disdain. After all we've been to prison.

But without us I believe they would never be here at

this time in a land that has changed where they can walk about freely unmolested. Unmolested by such forces as once might have roamed around to do them physical harm or such forces that I knew well that would just pick them up off the street and then beat them up then throw them in jail.

Many things have changed for the better, but I know myself and others like me, were very instrumental and influential in those changes. I'm tired and weary now, after a long struggle but I have finally come to realise. It's time to move on.

END